ABOUT GOD

ABOUT GOD

JOHN WEAVERSON

Troitsa Books
Huntington, New York

Editorial Production:	Susan Boriotti
Office Manager:	Annette Hellinger
Graphics:	Frank Grucci and Jennifer Lucas
Information Editor:	Tatiana Shohov
Book Production:	Patrick Davin, Cathy DeGregory, Donna Dennis, Jennifer Kuenzig, Christine Mathosian, Tammy Sauter and Lynette Van Helden
Circulation:	John Bakewell, Lisa DeGangi and Michael Pazy Mino

Library of Congress Cataloging-in-Publication Data

Weaverson, John.
    About God / by John Weaverson
        p.   cm.
    ISBN 1-56072-683-0
    1. God. I. Title.
BT102.W375   1999
231--dc21

99-14684
CIP

Copyright 2000 by John Weaverson
    Troitsa Books, a division of
    Nova Science Publishers, Inc.
    227 Main Street, Suite 100
    Huntington, New York 11743
    Tele. 631-424-6682   Fax 631-424-4666
    e-mail: Novascience@earthlink.net
    e-mail: Novascil@aol.com
    Web Site: http://www.nexusworld.com/nova

All rights reserved. No part of this book may be reproduced, stored in a retrieval system or transmitted in any form or by any means: electronic, electrostatic, magnetic, tape, mechanical photocopying, recording or otherwise without permission from the publishers.

The authors and publisher have taken care in preparation of this book, but make no expressed or implied warranty of any kind and assume no responsibility for any errors or omissions. No liability is assumed for incidental or consequential damages in connection with or arising out of information contained in this book.

This publication is designed to provide accurate and authoritative information with regard to the subject matter covered herein. It is sold with the clear understanding that the publisher is not engaged in rendering legal or any other professional services. If legal or any other expert assistance is required, the services of a competent person should be sought. FROM A DECLARATION OF PARTICIPANTS JOINTLY ADOPTED BY A COMMITTEE OF THE AMERICAN BAR ASSOCIATION AND A COMMITTEE OF PUBLISHERS.

Printed in the United States of America

Unless otherwise noted, all Scripture quotations are taken from the New Revised Standard Version of the Bible.

Dedicated to

John W. Carlton
(1920 – 1989)

Contents

Introduction		1
Chapter 1	Walking	3
Chapter 2	On Writing About God	5
Chapter 3	God Revealing God	7
Chapter 4	What God is Like	13
Chapter 5	God Delivering	19
Chapter 6	Tunnel	25
Chapter 7	God Believing in Us	27
Chapter 8	About God and Loneliness	31
Chapter 9	Made in the Image of God	37
Chapter 10	Answers in the Long Term	45
Chapter 11	Sin and Forgiveness	49
Chapter 12	Bad Relating / Prejudice	57
Chapter 13	Relating to God	63
Chapter 14	God's Presence	67
Chapter 15	God and Our Restless Spirit	69
Chapter 16	Magical Thinking of Prayers	75
Chapter 17	Difficult Times	81
Chapter 18	To Know God	85
Chapter 19	Made to be Human	91
Chapter 20	Jesus of Nazareth at One with God	99
Chapter 21	Spirit of God	105
Chapter 22	Uncertainties and Trust	113
Chapter 23	Access to Knowing	117
Chapter 24	2000 AD and Beyond	121
Chapter 25	Walking	137

INTRODUCTION

As God "looks down" upon us, upon our generations, upon our societies, upon our governments, upon our nations, God not only sees the consequences of our life's work, handiwork and all related results we have affected, but also down within the very depths of each of us as individuals. God looks in to the places inside a person where other people cannot see. Others cannot truly approach with any genuine confidence the true state of that inner realm of a person's being. There, deep within that private inner realm, lie the answers to profound questions regarding the love that there is toward others, or toward God, or to oneself. Human beings have developed a means of hiding those uniquely private, personal depths from others, keeping others from seeing very far within. We keep distance. The Creator God, however, looks in, views the depths which the Creator formed from our beginnings and actually beholds our most private, intimate and deepest yearnings. One cannot hide that inner part which is utterly and completely accessible to God. In looking down the Divine Being sees our relationship with God and beholds how that relationship shapes our lives.

As the all-righteous, Most Holy God, the Divine Being looks within the human being and withholds judgment, for now. Since now is always the time for wondrous love and divine caring, God loves us unconditionally, generously. Merciful love abounds. God loves to relate to us right there in that most private, intimate and deepest yearning place within each of us. God looks, and offers love. It is in this innermost context that we fully realize that God considers our relationships with others around us and with God.

May we move to a resolution in the most meaningful way that we can, one generated from that private, inner realm. Let us hope for those days when we human beings will actually and completely stop hurting each other physically, emotionally, or psychologically. We have, as a human race, committed sins against each other, large and small wrongdoings, every day of our existence. With Eternal God's help, we will eventually learn that it is in our own interest to behave civilly and fairly with others. We hurt ourselves when we hurt others — this we can admit is true. We all realize that hurt can penetrate deep inside us; we hurt deeply. Hurting is wrong. May we find God's help within each of us to actually arrive at the day when all hurting stops, when people stop hurting other people, once and for all, for good. Perhaps we will live to see the day when we will no longer find it necessary to voice the hope to others, "May the peace of God be with you" – for on that day of absolutely no hurting, we will all possess that peace of God already.

CHAPTER 1

WALKING

You are walking. You come alongside a fence which encloses a piece of wooded land which dips low enough for you to see the top of some of the trees there. Evidence of life abounds in front of you. You can see and hear this evidence. The effects of the soft breeze upon the branches are displayed in the gentle swaying of the leaves and proclaimed in their steady rustling noises. You sense you actually hear plant life. Then you realize this steady rustling is merely a backdrop, a constant background music for the intermittent sounds of various bird calls originating from somewhere within these trees. Then you know you also hear animal life. You enjoy coming along this fence; you have walked along it many times recently.

It's there – right there, through that section of branches that your attention is drawn! The leaves are a gathered mix of light and dark greens, those lightened by the sunlight and those darkened by shade from other leaves . . . a marbled mix of light and dark green coloring. You notice a small, delicate-looking bird building a nest at a narrow-wedged fork of a limb. You hear the sounds, too, of that activity. For several moments, you effortlessly witness that bird arrange its nest with short, tiny twigs, one at a time, carefully pressing each one down into its clump of twigs to securely fasten it all together. You now realize that even though you may have witnessed this kind of event before, you are truly focusing upon it as if it is your very first time. You convince yourself the nest is definitely enlarging minute by minute and obviously growing with sturdy construction as each short, tiny twig is brought in. You react, almost audibly, "How wonderful nature is! How interesting!"

Then you continue walking on further, but resolve to stop by the next day at this same spot when you will again walk along this fence.

You are walking. You come alongside that fence which encloses the piece of wooded land which dips low enough for you to see the top of some of the trees there. You usually enjoy coming along this fence, but a heavy rainstorm overnight with violent wind caused you to recall that little bird's handiwork and now you wonder if the new nest fared okay. Then you reach the same spot to peer through the same section of branches to find that exact place again. It's there . . . you locate that same narrow-wedged fork of a limb . . . but, there's no nest. It's gone. It's not there, nor is there any sight of it nearby. There are no sounds of activity either. Gone. There, your attention is drawn rather intently. But no matter how many moments you spend staring at that precise spot, there's simply no nest. You feared the effects of the night's rainstorm and the wind's fury. Thoughts shift slightly as you recall how you enjoyed yesterday viewing the delicate bird so industrious in its labor, carefully constructing its nest, pressing each short twig into the clump of twigs to securely fasten it all together. You remember how you resolved to stop by again at this same spot for you do enjoy coming alongside this fence. Your mind moves to thoughts of just what has become of that little bird. It's gone.

You continue walking.

CHAPTER 2

ON WRITING ABOUT GOD

Any author writing a book with such a title as *About God* could quickly be considered rather audacious, assuming, arrogant, presumptuous, brazen and foolish. We can feel such an author would surely expect readers to be too accepting of what a writer has to say. First of all, who could genuinely presume to really know all about God? Just who does this author think he is? The degree of audacity evidenced in such a book must be overwhelming, to be sure, to attempt to write material *about God*. These are all quite understandable reactions: we should exercise caution. Obviously, a certain degree of healthy skepticism should prove most useful for all readers of such books.

While acknowledging we owe so very much to so many who have gone before us, we can perhaps note we ourselves are certainly among many throughout the whole kingdom of God, which is comprised of joyous possessors and tormented seekers. Possibly, we all during our lifetimes are both joyous possessors and tormented seekers. Experiences in our lives do vary. From this context of life's ambiguities we all arise to give prayers up to God, as we give support to others or simply offer anything which may prove helpful spiritually. We do these knowingly and unknowingly from childhood on, at least with some degree of involvement: a word of encouragement here, or a simple glancing smile there, go a long way to assist others in their own ordeals of life, whether major ones or minor ones at any particular time.

In a sense, everything we do and say in our lives can ultimately be connected in some way back to God – as all our life's goals for good, our intentions for family members, our dreams, fears and thoughts all in some way and at some basic level point back to God. These say much about God, about the relationship we each have individually with God, and what we hope about God. In short, one might even make a case that all of life is about God, since life began with the Creator God – so we are all related, so to speak, to God: we are God's creation, like it or not. Our life's journey from moment of birth to moment of death is a journey of discovery of who we are, as made in the image of God the creator – such that in some strangely wonderful way, some goodness of the Creator is reflected in that which the Creator created, that is, in us as human beings. So much of what we are, want to be, can be and will be in the final analysis is actually all intertwined as the created is with the creator, our God. It is in this intertwining context that this created being of God offers some observations, thoughts and ideas about the Creator God. Should any material in this book prove beneficial in any way to just one fellow seeker's faith in God, then it can be rightly deemed successful and good, and as a consequence, about God's work . . . and about God.

CHAPTER 3

GOD REVEALING GOD

How can we human beings come to some understanding of what God is all about – a deity who is infinitely above humans in countless ways and seemingly overwhelming to comprehend? How can we fathom such a great, majestic deity who is infinitely holy, righteous, loving, etc.? To attempt to gain some understanding of deity, God, we first need to realize that God revealed much of what we have come to know about God in actual historical events. God entered history in order to reveal the divine to us in a more direct way. If history is generally defined as our recording of past events, then surely we can affirm that God is not only an historical Being, but really pre-historical as well – for certainly we can affirm that Eternal God predated any recording humans ever made. Science informs us that humans began late in the sequence of created life: so, God is surely prehistoric Being, as well. In believing God to be eternal, actually even before time itself, we best begin any attempts at understanding at some far, distant point – as far back as we can go. We can remember the beginning words of Genesis, the very first book arranged in the Old Testament, "In the beginning God . . . ." Perhaps we might start there.

One contemporary philosopher's views on a theology of how the world was created includes the following points of Christian belief: there is a distinction between God and the universe since God, the creator of all things, is considered to be before all things created. "The Genesis stories of creation make it clear that the world has a *beginning*. Because it has a beginning, it is not eternal. This means it is not ultimate. God, its Maker, who is without beginning or end, is ultimate."[1]

With this starting point as our basis, we can consider our attempts "to understand" as opposed to "fully comprehend." Since we humans were not there at the very beginning we must make do with what notions or ideas we can fathom with our own human efforts. The universe began without us; Creator God started the universe without us; these things we accept, as we have little choice in the matter.

> God is distinguished from the universe. God has no beginning but is everlasting. As Creator of the universe, God is not part of the universe nor is it a part of God. Creation depends on God for its existence.

> God . . . acts freely and thus is inherently stable and inherently full, complete, or perfect. The act of creation is thus an act of sheer generosity. God's freedom in creation is the reason we view creation as an act of sheer generosity. . . . A being who is complete in essence, who is inexhaustibly rich, lacking nothing, is beyond our comprehension.

> Nonetheless, we have some understanding of God. Because the world begins and God does not, and because God makes the world freely, God is rich and full. . . . We understand that God is perfect (complete and full) because God created the world freely, and we can understand that even though we do not *comprehend* the perfection of divine being. . . . We know God, therefore, not in essence but only in relation to us. It is because God makes a world and relates to us in other ways that we gain some understanding of deity.[2]

God reveals the divine to us: the Christian tradition holds that God reveals first through the divine act of creating the world and all that is in it; and then later, through self-revelation to the early people of an ancient Israel; and then later still, of course, to later Israel and beyond through the work and person of Jesus as Christ. In other words, God reveals *before* the history of the world and also *in* the history of the world in which we all live. As far as the prehistory is concerned, we can read a translation of the very first words of the first book arranged in the Old Testament, words possibly meant to convey

---

[1] Diogenes Allen, *Philosophy for Understanding Theology* (Atlanta: John Knox Press, 1985) 1.
[2] Allen 2, 10, 11.

vivid imagery before human beings were witnesses: "In the beginning when God created the heavens and the earth, the earth was a formless void and darkness covered the face of the deep . . ." (Genesis 1:1-2). Later we know God revealed to the faces of humankind. The early, ancient account of Moses as the most prominent early figure in Hebrew and Christian faiths provides an interesting example. Moses' encounter with God has been considered in Christian traditions a truly ultimate, inner experience of a revealing deity, a genuine knowing of God's presence – though still a God really incomprehensible to human minds.

The book of Exodus (3:1-15) provides that ancient rendering of the revealing God to a human mind. Here, God also reveals God's name. The human mind that this is revealed to, in this case, is of Moses, the legendary figure but real nonetheless, and God revealed much including God's name to him. Today it is generally well accepted that Moses lived in the thirteenth century BC, a time of nomadic tribal existence, when inhabitants moved about often according to the feeding needs of their flocks of animals. This account tells us Moses was merely preoccupied with his daily, routine task of tending flocks of sheep. This setting was said to be upon a mountain, complete with the appearance of a bush all afire but not actually consumed by it; such a strong symbol given by the ancient writer provides us with the image of undeniably powerful divine presence appearing before a humble human being – in this instance, someone just tending sheep. Regarding the name God gives out, the disclosure of one's name in ancient times tended to mean a self-disclosure of one's very person, a real giving of something significant to someone else. So, for divine God to do this, it could very well seem as if God was making a declaration of God's innermost being! From Exodus 3:13-14:

> But Moses said to God, "If I come to the Israelites and say to them, 'The God of your ancestors has sent me to you,' and they ask me, 'What is his name?' what shall I say to them?"
>
> God said to Moses, "I AM WHO I AM." He said further, "This you shall say to the Israelites, 'I AM has sent me to you'."

Prior to this encounter the name associated with God was well rooted in the ancient religious life of the early ancestors – in fact, it was almost always referred to as "God of Abraham, Isaac, and Jacob." Of course, this understanding underlines a relationship with Moses' ancestors, or fathers, before him, thus conveying the relational continuance of the God of history throughout their lifetimes. This new encounter with Moses meant this was the same God, now also the God of Moses, and the God now revealing God's being in a new manner – God as bearer both of the old and new divine names. Thus the new name marks a transition from the past to the then-present. However, the biblical account is brief. As it has been considered by countless theologians with much debate over the centuries, the verbal phrase "I AM WHO I AM" is deemed to be based on the Hebrew verb "to be." As it appears in the Hebrew text, the phrase could be translated in more than one way! The acceptable renderings are "I am who I am," or "I will be who I will be," or "I will be what I will be." Probably the initial human response nowadays to this name, whichever one, would be to sense a certain vagueness or hiddenness of God, rather than an actual self-disclosure. Apparently God is disclosing vagueness! Yes, God's presence was assured, very definitely, but God's self-revelation has such a vague quality to it as to prompt us to wish for a further elaboration, or more.

> Self-revelation has such fluidity about it as to permit a continual unfolding of the divine nature without exhausting the total content of God's nature. Rather than being able to define God with such precision as to capture the totality of his presence, the phrase reveals the nature of God while allowing the possibility of further insight and revelation. Although continually present as a God who does not change, he is at the same time present in every generation with new connotations and implications.[3]

In our attempts to view God as a self-revealing deity, we probably should admit our utter inability to capture God in a thorough definition onto paper. As God is limitless, God is not bound by human words which would do exactly that – bind and limit. Attempts to gather specifics will perhaps continue to falter as the subject defies any specific limits. God is limitless and continually present to us all. It would seem that throughout all humankind's history of relating with God, God was indeed available. In addition, God is changeless: God is a God without change, in that God's character simply does not change, God's ways do not change, and God's purposes do not change. In

---

[3] Roy L. Honeycutt, Jr., "Exodus," *The Broadman Bible Commentary*, ed. Clifton J. Allen, vol. 1 (Nashville: Broadman Press, 1973) 315-316.

this context, we may better understand that God is as God is, or maybe *not changing*, or as the Hebrew rendering had it in God's self-revealing name, "I AM WHO I AM," or "I WILL BE WHO I WILL BE." Probably we should leave it at that.

As for God's unbounded nature, God's limitless essence can overwhelm our understanding completely. Notions of unlimitedness are baffling. We humans are bound by time and place, and we have limitations of power and knowledge. God, on the other hand, is not bound by time since God is above time, having made all of creation and the very system of time: God's being is eternal, before time actually. God is also not bound by place nor any limits of power or knowledge. These kinds of thoughts can be staggering to our human minds. But now we add to this the very fact that this Eternal God, the timeless God, has chosen to reveal God's self to us *in time* – at a specific place in the timestream, a specific place in history. This is where we have to understand that even though God's nature is changeless, Creator God is not static in the active relationship with all the created beings God loves. As we recall that God chose to reveal God not only in the acts of creation itself before recorded history, and then later in the revealing acts in the relationship with faithful ancient Israel's ancestors, we furthermore consider God revealing in newer ways in the timeline, as we can visualize it, in the work and person of Jesus as Christ some 2,000 years ago.

God was not static in the relationship with human beings: not with the very early faithful, not with the person of Christ, and further still, not with the faithful persons of today. God has not been static in relating. God has chosen to reveal God to us – and since we are creatures bound in time, God chose to break into our time in order to reveal. Just how did God reveal God, to humans then and now? As this is so difficult to comprehend adequately, we can only accept it in similar fashion in the vague manner God puts it: God reveals as God reveals. God relates as God relates. God is as God is.

Chapter 4

What God is Like

We have now briefly considered some of how God has revealed God. We note that God has revealed from the very beginning. Even through such times in which God has appeared to reveal in a vague or indefinite way, human beings have been observing. Over the centuries the Creator God's created beings have learned much about their Maker. Through our individual faith relationships with our personal God, many have come to believe we do in fact know God. We have also yearned to know more *about* God, as we wonder and reflect upon God's character. Human beings seem to desire much more than mere acknowledgement, "God is as God is." We all appear to yearn for more about God. In turning our attention now towards a description of the character of God, we naturally tend to list attributes, since our human minds find this an easier way to understand characteristics of a personal being — in this case, even a divine one.

In attempting to focus upon a more specific way of viewing God, we initially must admit one significant difficulty: no human description of God can truly be sufficient because the subject is simply too vast. It is certainly an arduous task to capture the total essence of the eternal, Divine Being in words. However, no other subject compels human thinking so. As human beings believe God to be a fact, a reality we encounter in the experience of life, we realize our minds turn to God's spiritual realm. Oftentimes, we reflect upon God's divine character in similar fashion as we would in human relationships here on earth. We appear to reflect upon attributes of God when we consider God's being. To this point in our discussion, we have invariably touched upon some attributes of God already and will unavoidably discuss many indirectly throughout the rest of this book, as we reflect upon God's being with our lifelong relationships with God and with others. To deal with human concerns with God we necessarily happen upon the very character of this personal God's being. (Much of this book addresses the subject of God's attributes, although it is of primary concern in chapter 9 and the latter chapters 19, 20 and 21.) Simply put, we cannot avoid, even should we want to, aspects of personal characteristics for God since our conception of God frames our human understanding of our experiences of God in our lives.

Now in moving to focus upon specific attributes of God's character, we may be required to take into account an aspect of our relating to God with which human beings have been confronted from our beginnings. This is the mystery of God, and it stands before our attempts to specify more about God. The mystery of God has been a reality of our humankind's ancient past and continues to our present day. We must resolutely acknowledge God's mystery as a caution to be heeded in any activity to arrive at specific and concrete definitions. As we remember the old story of God's revelation to Moses of the divine name, "I AM WHO I AM," we are compelled to accept that divine response as a truly vague self-disclosure. God, for God's own reasons and purposes, chose to reveal the name of God in this very unrevealing manner, a name actually hidden in an obvious lack of clarity. From this biblical account human beings could surmise that a reason for this disclosure is that it tells us all we really need to know about God — nothing more is needed, this is sufficient. We recall questions from the Old Testament book of Job (11:7 New English Bible): "Can you fathom the mystery of God? Can you fathom the perfection of the Almighty?" Another biblical translation renders the larger passage (11:5-9 New Revised Standard Version) in the following way.

> But oh, that God would speak, and open his lips to you, and that he would tell you the secrets of wisdom! For wisdom is many-sided. Know then that God exacts of you less than your guilt deserves.
>
> Can you find out the deep things of God? Can you find out the limit of the Almighty? It is higher than heaven — what can you do? Deeper than Sheol — what can you know? Its measure is longer than the earth, and broader than the sea.

Human experiences with God over the many centuries as well as our own individual dealings with God (through times of struggle, for example) also point to another expression of God's relating to us. A personal God, the Creator of us all who yearns for ever closer relationships with God's created beings, surely understands the human yearning to seek God, to reach out for God, and to know as much as possible about God. A psalmist's voice offered these words, "As a deer longs for flowing streams, so my soul longs for you, O God. My soul thirsts for God, for the living God. When shall I come and behold the face of God?" (Psalm 42:1-2). In all probability, we seek more of God because we already know some things about God; what we know in our hearts compels us to seek more. We desire much more; God understands this. Even taking into account the great mystery of God, there are indeed some aspects of God's being, which we have learned from our experiencing God, which indicate much of what God is like — even if the mystery of God "is longer than the earth, and broader than the sea."

There are many attributes that we can list which certainly pertain to God. Some appear more significant than others; some we are more acquainted with than others; a few seem familiar; others, obscure. At this point we can consider those attributes which appear to reveal the main thrust of God's being, as God relates to us. In this context it could well be argued that of the numerous attributes for God's character, the singular attribute fitting God's expression to us is derived from the brief scriptural statement, "God is love."

If the first and foremost attribute of God in a compilation of characteristics is that God is loving, it might be observed that from love came God's activity of creation of all life in the first place. The Christian view is that from the context of love God created everything that was created. From love, God created us in God's own image, giving us life and the great possibility for eternal life with this loving God. From love, God broke into our time and place some 2,000 years ago in human form, as the incarnate Jesus as Christ. Certainly this was the most uniquely magnificent expression of the depths of divine love for God's created humanity! We can also note that Christ in his day summarized the much earlier *Ten* Commandments (which were intended as the rule or guide for proper, healthy, good living) into *two* directives: Love the Lord your God with all your heart and with all your soul and with all your mind; Love your neighbor as yourself. It is clear that as these guides were born in the context of love, Christ expresses the aspect of love as the underlying foundation in God's guidance for proper relationships with God and with others. So, it is our understanding that we live . . . with love. Our personal, loving God provides us wondrous love and divine care. God, knowing us intimately, loves us. Even when we sin and disappoint God, God loves us still; of course, God does not love our sins or our sinfulness, but God does continue to love us, unconditionally and generously. God is love.

As wondrous as this divine love appears to the human heart, the concept of a loving God has real complications for many. Unfortunately, the human mind witnesses the vast amounts of suffering in the world and struggles to weigh evidence in consideration of that age-old problem: how does a loving God permit such occurrences of crippling or deadly diseases, terrible tragedies, accidents, acts of violence, etc. to happen in this world? Also, many of us realize all too well how the anguished grief of experiencing the loss of a loved one tests our faith in God. Is God really loving?

This problem of human suffering has probably been with us always; it is certainly most troubling. It has been much debated with seemingly sufficient evidence on both sides. Of course, even with this somber awareness of darkness in life, we likewise are quite well aware of countless moments of light: times of joy, laughter, love, hope and peace within our lives. These do occur; they are not merely imagined. The human mind may, however, attempt to weigh the dark to the light in some quantitative manner, to determine the answer to the problem of suffering in our world. Hopefully, a loving God is above it all. Since none of us can truly solve this satisfactorily, we might resign ourselves to leave it unresolved, to deal with it the best we can, or in other words, to simply live with it. It may just be a matter likened to the example of the half-glass of water: some describe it positively as half-full, some describe it negatively as half-empty. Individual interpretation is the key. After all the arguments of debate are recast, reworked and presented, and after all emotions are truly spent and exhausted, the actual resolution of this problem of suffering in a loving God's world is finally left to each individual believer — not to a great scholar of the fine points of law, but to each of us, to you and to me. We, each in our own behalf individually, will somehow arrive upon the deciding moment: is it true that "God is love" or not?

In our judgement of the love of God, we may need to remember that our love is connected, or related, to God's love. In addition, it is extremely easy to miss the bit of light sometimes, when all seems so dark around us: we can easily fail to feel loving or to feel loved. Moreover, we may recall that through love God chose to come into this world in human flesh, in Jesus as Christ: surely, the eternal, Holy God did not have to do this at all. Jesus suffered and died on the cross in a most painful, anguished manner; we can fully accept that God shared with us even in the suffering of death itself. Our personal God understands the darkness. God's active involvement working within the world through God's spirit within us (rather than working from outside of the world) can encourage us and accompany us. This same eternal God, right here with us, is our companion whether in times of felt-loss or felt-love. Our loving God knows both, as we human beings know both. Since we and God are related, our love is connected as well. A scripture passage which touches upon this love is 1 John 4:7-8: "Let us love one another, because love is from God; everyone who loves is born of God and knows God. Whoever does not love does not know God, for God is love." Finally, we can affirm that from love, God created us in God's own image, giving us life and the real possibility for eternal life with this loving God. This appears to be wondrous love, to the human mind as well as to the human heart.

As we move beyond the principal attribute of love, we discover other essential aspects of what God is like. Briefly listed, they include the following: God is spirit; God is eternal; and God is creator. Again, the character of God's being is considered throughout much of the book and these attributes as well as others are developed along in the material ahead as we reflect upon our relationships with God and with other relationships here on earth. In addition, God has historically been deemed omnipresent, omnipotent and omniscient, meaning respectively all-present, all-powerful and all-knowing. Also, God is personal, holy, righteous, just, merciful, and infinite. Moreover our God is deemed to be actively involved in various roles in relationships with God's created beings. The Church has also accepted God as a triune being, or three persons in one substance, namely: God the Father, God the Son (Jesus as Christ) and God the Holy Spirit. We can conclude this discussion for the time being stating that all of these attributes and terms for God can contribute to our faith and understanding of the divine God's character. Yet God is not limited to any finite terminology of human beings (again, see chapters 9, 19, 20 and 21). Verbal renderings, though if offered in just reverence and acknowledgement of the mystery of God, can edify our understanding of a usable conception of God.

Ultimately, God is the God which we individually experience within, during the various highs and lows of life: the personal God to whom we rush in prayer in anguished moments, and the God in whom we confide as we share our hopes, dreams and aspirations seeking acceptance, agreement and assistance from God. We relate to God. We experience God. We reflect about God.

"As a deer longs for flowing streams, so my soul longs for you, O God."

CHAPTER 5

GOD DELIVERING

Apparently sometime during the earliest days of human life on earth, a perspective formed of a great God "out there" or "up there." With extremely poor ideas of science available, early human beings saw God as incredibly awesome in the use of divine power partly because of the effects of severe weather – such as the storm's fury causing lightning, which in turn caused fire; or rains causing floods; or droughts causing seasons of blight, famine, or disease. Life could be very, very hard. God was all-powerful – of this there was no doubt whatsoever.

There is an account in ancient Hebrew history, in the Old Testament book of Daniel, which provides us with a tense view of a particular crisis requiring action by the all-powerful God of the believers. The passage describes an extremely dire situation which tested the faith of the Hebrew people. The setting points to a peculiar life-threatening moment of decision for three Hebrews professing their faithfulness only to God. The three were directed to give absolute allegiance to the ruler's idol god; they were threatened by the king of Babylonia, Nebuchadnezzar, to comply with his commands to bow down and worship a golden idol or else die in a fiery furnace. Such a dilemma, forced upon them by way of terror, gave them a moment for a decision. Their response was presented this way by the biblical writer, in Daniel 3:16-18:

> Shadrach, Meshach, and Abednego answered the king, "O Nebuchadnezzar, we have no need to present a defense to you in this matter. If our God whom we serve is able to deliver us from the furnace of blazing fire and out of your

hand, O king, let him deliver us. But if not, be it known to you, O king, that we will not serve your gods and we will not worship the golden statue that you have set up."

The response of these Hebrews to such a crisis, in which they found themselves caught, points up several aspects of their faith in God. First of all, they pronounced their views in an apparent mix of steadfastness and daring, as their tremendous courage in the face of such a dilemma was evident for others to witness. Their words conveyed their belief that 1) the all-powerful God was able to deliver them from that ordeal, and 2) if God did not deliver them from that situation of terror they would still remain faithful to their God only, and not to whatever the king demanded of them, regardless of the consequences (death by fire). Their faith in God exhibited a strength which fashioned their moral will resolute. Yes, they were determined to do what they believed to be right, to uphold their fidelity to their God – and even if God did not save them from their predicament of terror, to compel themselves to the situation, trusting their future to the hands of God.

The ancient account of these Hebrew faithful is certainly of a time and place removed from our society and culture today. It seems many, many centuries removed from where we are now. We may even ask whether any such dire situation could occur in today's world.

Born in 1906, a son of a German professor of psychiatry, Dietrich Bonhoeffer studied theology first in Berlin and later in New York. As Adolf Hitler was rising to power in 1933, Bonhoeffer, a student chaplain and university lecturer in Berlin, began to realize possible dangers to the Church in Germany. A prolific writer, the theologian Bonhoeffer had focused on the suffering Jesus Christ and became known for his views of Christ as "there only for others." Bonhoeffer also spoke out on the nature of the Christian community. His work increasingly included challenges to Christians of his own day to reject complacent, undisciplined faith in their lives. As Hitler grew ever more powerful, Bonhoeffer became known as one of a group of anti-Nazi pastors in Germany's "church struggle." In 1935 he was appointed head of a seminary; Hitler's government, however, closed the seminary two years later.[4] As freedoms began to deteriorate in his country, he soon found

---

[4] Ruth Zerner, "Dietrich Bonhoeffer," *Eerdman's Handbook to the History of Christianity*, ed. Tim Dowley (Grand Rapids: Wm. B. Eerdman's Publishing Co.,

that he was forbidden by the Nazi authorities to teach. This widely known theologian then traveled more, visiting England and the United States. In 1939, upon completion of a lecture tour in the United States, he was urged by many friends not to return to Germany. After all, the European war appeared unavoidable to most; Nazi Germany was a menacing threat to those both within and outside its borders, and the United States, of course, was an ocean away. The Nazi government continued to mass powers and exert tighter controls:

> The most important was that of governing by emergency decree. This was the end of parliament and parliamentary sovereignty. Armed with these powers, the Nazis proceeded to carry out a revolutionary destruction of democratic institutions. By 1939, there was virtually no sector of German society not controlled or intimidated by them.[5]

Despite deterioration of the Germany he knew before Hitler, and despite the urging of many friends, Bonhoeffer wished to return. He rejected the possibility of a job in the United States and was convinced he had to face the extreme hardships ahead with his fellow Christians in Germany. As he was the proponent of the theological notion of the suffering Jesus Christ as "there only for others," Bonhoeffer was convinced following Christ's example was the Christian duty; he felt compelled to be with his fellow German Christians in their time of dire need. So at peace in the rightness of his courageous decision, he would later write that upon his trip back to his homeland he sensed a distinct inner peace. The fears expressed by many proved true as Germany suffered further political oppression and attacks upon the religious community. Ever-tightening restrictions and limitations were placed on the churches by the controlling Nazi government. The harsh realities of his day required so much from those faithful to God, as the country became a place of severe testing. Bonhoeffer's theological work of challenging Christians to reject complacent, undisciplined faith in their lives was soon put to the test in the most severe ways. Bonhoeffer himself was said to have done all he could in the face of a formidable crush liberally used by the Nazi government. In

---

1982), 603.

[5] J. M. Roberts, *History of the World* (New York: Oxford University Press Inc., 1993), 763.

1943 he was arrested because of his involvement in smuggling fourteen Jews off to Switzerland for their survival. We should note his personal testing was particularly apt as he had authored in 1937 *The Cost of Discipleship*, emphasizing the importance of people stepping out and following Christ in costly discipleship. As it happened, his was costly also. Yet from his prison cell Bonhoeffer continued to write; it was from prison that he would write his most popular works, later published as *Letters and Papers from Prison*. Realizing he might face the sentence of death, the act of following Christ's example of being there for others meant a tremendous cost – life itself. Severe difficulties were ever present; his daily ordeal, great indeed. He wrote much, including, "O God, early in the morning do I cry unto Thee. Help me to pray and to think only of Thee. I cannot pray alone. In me there is darkness. But with Thee there is light."[6]

In his prison letters Bonhoeffer explored pathways of future church renewal. He also struggled to remain focused upon the Christian hope: words written to help others' struggles were no doubt still a part of his days, even there, at that place. The imprisoned theologian wrote for others' benefit to help bolster their faith:

> I believe that God can and will bring good out of evil, even out of the greatest evil. . . . I believe that God will give us all the strength we need to help us to resist in all times of distress. But he never gives it in advance, lest we should rely on ourselves and not on him alone. A faith such as this should allay all our fears for the future.[7]

One Sunday in April, 1945, after leading a small worship service with fellow prisoners in Flossenburg Prison, Bonhoeffer was summoned by the guards. He was executed by hanging. He was thirty-nine.

Words may again reach our hearing. "God . . . is able to deliver us from the furnace of blazing fire. . . . But if not, be it known to you, O king, that we will not serve your gods." We recall Dietrich Bonhoeffer's few words, "In me there is darkness. But with Thee there is light." Other later writers add these thoughts.

---

[6] Dietrich Bonhoeffer, *Letters and Papers from Prison*, ed. Eberhard Bethge (London: SCM Press Ltd., 1986), 139.

Relationship with God through Christ brings us a life which death cannot extinguish. . . . Death still holds its mysteries. "What we will be has not yet been made known," John says. But "now we are children of God" (1 John 3:2). It is confidence in our relationship with God, and in His great gift of eternal life, which makes the experience of death different for the believer. We do not view death as any less an enemy, for death is God's enemy, too. But we are able to see death as a defeated enemy. We realize that "if we live, we live to the Lord; and if we die, we die to the Lord. So, whether we live or die, we belong to the Lord" (Romans 14:8). The fact that death cannot threaten our relationship with God is the key to a Christian approach to death and dying. We need not welcome death, or even be calm in its presence. We can acknowledge our fears, our disappointments, all the uncertainty associated with meeting any enemy face to face. And we can still find great comfort and assurance in God's personal commitment to us as His children: ". . . neither death nor life, neither angels nor demons, neither the present nor the future, nor any powers, neither height nor depth, nor anything else in all creation, will be able to separate us from the love of God that is in Christ Jesus our Lord" (Romans 8:38-39).[8]

---

[7] Bonhoeffer, 11.
[8] Larry Richards and Paul Johnson, M.D., *Death and the Caring Community* (Portland, OR: Multnomah Press, 1980), 31.

CHAPTER 6

TUNNEL

At times, life can seem to be just like walking through a long darkened tunnel. Indeed, it is a really long tunnel, and it appears very dark there. We so much want to use the sense of sight, but we cannot see anything. We all, in fact, depend a great deal on seeing our way, yet at that place it is so dark. We conclude we are forced, seemingly against our will, to use the sense of touch instead, in order to move along through the tunnel. But walking is so difficult. Very quickly we realize that walking becomes more like stumbling and bumping clumsily into things . . . sometimes we get so frustrated, start complaining, maybe grow angry in outbursts, or seem depressed with it all. Questions come . . . is this what life consists of? Is this what life is all about? Why can't we see what is ahead? We seek answers: it seems no satisfying answers are found. After a good bit of time, while stumbling along and bumping over things in the way, suddenly we think we detect a light, a small point of light far ahead. Did it just appear? After a while, we wonder if it actually might have been there all along as our eyes perhaps were not fully adjusted to the darkness to pick out such a small bit of light. We know human eyes require a period of adjusting. Probably, it just takes time.

Life, we begin to hope, offers this light, however small, far ahead to walk toward. Maybe this is in fact what life is somehow about: walking toward light . . . and doing this in a seemingly dark and confining place like a tunnel. But suddenly there comes a light . . . or was it there all along? Faith is hoping that the light looms much larger, feels more present, and shines more radiantly at the very end, the source. We all hope. It is easy to wonder at times if we are being forced to touch all along throughout our way; we cannot see very well in the dark. We keep walking. We keep walking. Probably, it just takes time.

"Now faith is the assurance of things hoped for, the conviction of things not seen" (Hebrews 11:1-2).

CHAPTER 7

GOD BELIEVING IN US

Our world was somehow formed long, long ago. Ages and ages ago, before our ancient ancestors were living on this planet, the whole universe came into being. In some way that even the most knowledgeable of present-day scientists are still not truly certain of, the world was created. How did this happen, and why? We can ask puzzling questions. Did the Creator God start this great, cosmic and magnificent grand creative experiment for divine amusement? Realizing how human history contains countless, horrible examples of cruel inhumanity upon ourselves, whether by a person toward another person, or by a group toward another group, or by a nation toward another nation, we might even dare to wonder if we have been quite entertaining to some great witness above it all. Surely we might conclude our existence on earth has at least been interesting. We can also ask, "Were we somehow placed here to live our lives amid a troubled world of immensely impossible odds just to survive?" We question things we do not understand. Questions come easily, as easily as difficulties come. Pain, suffering and death have always been around us, in our ancestors' past and in our present.

Human beings have, however, for the most part survived the trials of living together. We can note and list numerous advances and accomplishments over the centuries which have stirred our collective hopes and human spirits. A few specific ones would include obvious progress in areas of education, health and medicines, personal safety, provision of shelter in better built housing, agricultural advances providing sufficient food in turn allowing improved nutrition, and keener awareness of the significance of human rights. Thankfully, such a list can be lengthened still, due to numerous technological strides in our era.

However, to be true to ourselves and to our total history, we regrettably must also recognize such achievements as developing "better" weapons — assorted guns, bombs and land mines, missiles, military aircraft, vessels, tanks as well as numerous other supplementary supplies necessary for military hardware in a "modern" warfare arsenal. Methods for securing destruction and death have progressed from mere hands, stones and sticks to our modern nuclear, chemical and biological methods, with even newer means no doubt presently "on the drawing board." Such horrific instances of human "progress" on our planet have shaped our human consciousness and self-awareness knowingly and unknowingly in our living through frequent periods of pain, suffering and death, from our ancestors' time to our own time today.

It is in this context that we may recall old voices saying 1) the universe has not always existed and it will not exist forever in its present form, and 2) the universe has not come into being by mere chance, as it was created by a personal God and is continually held in being by God. God surely started "this grand experiment" of creation, and pronounced it as good. Also, God provided human beings with personal freedoms to choose between right and wrong, not treating us as mere puppets on strings doing exactly what and when the master puppeteer wishes. Generally speaking, humans are personally free. With our God-given freedoms to choose and to determine our courses of actions, the progress of good and the progress of bad may nevertheless be said to be in some sort of balance. There are times the great scale has seemed to tilt a little one way and other times tilt the other way, but generally it could be said, it appears to be in some sort of balance.

How does this impact our faith? It is in this context in which we presently find ourselves living that we encounter consideration of our basic beliefs and their implications upon others around us. Whatever world view we individually may hold and whatever religion or faith we fervently ascribe to, most of us have deep questions regarding where our future is leading us.

We all may also wonder how a Creative God is involved in all of this. In addition, we can admit we each may wonder how our own selves will respond in life ahead, as we surely have doubts about how many other people around us will respond. With so many questions, we can turn to the meaning of it all. Just possibly we all, each and every one of us, might be somehow and some way ready to accept that we were not simply placed here on earth to live our lives amid a troubled world of immensely impossible odds just to survive. One answer could involve love. The Creator God created us all in love, for love and companionship with God: so by loving God, we may be more gentle toward others around us, even those we do not agree with and possibly those we may believe we really do not like at all. Actually, we might conclude God believed in us, by God's act of creating us. God believed in us by giving us genuine freedoms of choice in our daily lives; we can assume God believes that with the gentle spirit of love and peace toward others we will arrive at good choices over bad ones, in turn resulting in peaceful outcomes and away from hurtful ones. With a rule of peace toward all, we may create among ourselves peace on earth — surely this is not an impossible goal, if only we include God within our basic moral viewpoints. If life indeed has some purpose and meaning after all, then certainly they can be found with loving peace in our hearts toward God and among ourselves. We can conclude the Creator God fashioned us to love God by choice and reflect the character of the loving God toward others, serving others in loving peace and enjoying God's creation of the world by caring for it as God's stewards. Long ago the apostle Paul wrote these words to an early group of Christians (from Philippians 4:4-9):

> Rejoice in the Lord always, again I will say Rejoice, let your gentleness be known to everyone. The Lord is near. Do not worry about anything, but in everything by prayer and supplication with thanksgiving let your requests be made known to God. And the peace of God, which surpasses all understanding, will guard your hearts and your minds in Christ Jesus. Finally, beloved, whatever is true, whatever is honorable, whatever is just, whatever is pure, whatever is pleasing, whatever is commendable, if there is any excellence and if there is anything worthy of praise, think about these things. Keep on doing the things that you have learned and received and heard and seen in me, and the God of peace will be with you.

If we can turn toward our God of peace, we can turn away from those countless instances of cruel hostilities shown in our past — a mean spirit exhibited either by one person toward another person, or by one group toward another group, or by one nation toward another nation. Our history of conflicts which cause pain, suffering and death to others need not continue as it has; we can indeed survive the trials of living together. It is possible. The

Creator God of peace, the God of love, began the creative experiment of life in this world for a serious reason — quite a Godly love was going on in our behalf. That was our beginning. Today, the quality of our lives is at stake, as are our very lives themselves — the spiritual life of us all has always been at stake right here on earth, right here in our very own communities, even in our own individual homes. "Peace begins with me," one can utter; peace begins at home, with each of us . . . possibly, *this* is precisely where we may acknowledge that God believes in us, for God gave us the freedom to choose in our decisions and actions within our control, aspects of our lives with those the closest to us. "Peace begins with me."

May the peace of God be with you.

CHAPTER 8

ABOUT GOD AND LONELINESS

There are many things we can say about our Creator God. However, we fully realize we cannot provide proof and concrete explanations regarding the divine Holy Being from the human perspective. This we must admit to ourselves right away. Today it has been said that "no proof is given of the Creator." This is because God dwells outside all human explanations: our God as such is not an explanation to be put down definitively onto paper, or listed in concrete terms — rather, God is a reality to be confronted. God will simply not be bound by human explanations.[9] The idea is of course more of experiencing *a relationship with God*. The reality of relating is far different than providing proof, concrete explanations and a binding of God into finite and limiting words. More importance is placed upon *relating* with God, our own Creator. Hopefully we can resist the tendency to rush to flatly pronounce, as in presenting such statements as "God is _____," but instead pause to consider, reflect and wonder "about God." Actually human limitations prevent brash, irresponsible pronouncements on our part regarding concrete explanations of the divine Holy Being. We do know we can discuss many aspects of God since we have over time learned much through observations of the human experience of relating with God. So, we can discuss many aspects *"about God's"* goodness, holiness, majesty and greatness. We can wonder in awe *about God* being personal with each individual, and yet realize God is unbounded measure, immense and vast. All

---

[9] James Houston, "In the Beginning, God," *Eerdman's Handbook to Christian Belief*, ed. Robin Keeley (Grand Rapids: Wm. B. Eerdman's Publishing Co., 1982), 210.

these things and more we can say *about God*. Numerous other religious matters, it should be stressed, are probably best left to the individual's personal faith with God.

Even so, one bold, blunt statement can be offered here about the creator role of God: the Creator God, we believe, created all things. We do know from science that before human beings walked on this earth many other species of animals moved about, existing here alongside the plant world. As plants and other living organisms were quite abundant on this planet well before humankind, we obviously conclude the Creator God first fashioned the vast variety of all other creatures, or living beings, along with all plant life, and then much later (many, many centuries apparently) created humans. We can say that these things we indeed know — yet, do we know "why" humans were created? Since it is often easy to imagine the being of God in personal human terms, we might imagine the Creator God initially surrounded by the majestic and great creation of early animal and plant life — and we may just wonder aloud if God was lonely! If we accept that God is personal and also loving and caring, we might be able to consider that God was lonely before humankind was created, with only impersonal animals and plants about. If God did make human beings in the divine image, the question could be raised, "Why did God create us?" Surely God did not have to introduce humans into the created world at all, as there was indeed a vast and diverse array of life here already. We can believe the idea behind our creation in God's own image (both then and now) was "that humanity has been created for a special relationship with God, intended to be personal and eternal." To believe we have our own individual personal relationship with an eternal God indeed positions us greatly above all other life in our world. It is in this context God most likely intended for us to live life fully in the divine presence, developing spiritually, mentally and morally as children of Creator God on whom God delights to pour divine love.[10]

As created children, upon reflection we realize our relatedness to the Creator and behold ways we may reflect God's love to others. As scripture teaches that we were made for fellowship with God, we might come to accept that we can find true self-expression and meaningful purpose only when we

---

[10] George Carey, "Made in the Image of God," *Eerdman's Handbook to Christian Belief*, ed. Robin Keeley (Grand Rapids: Wm. B. Eerdman's Publishing Co., 1982), 220.

find and enjoy God's personal relationship of love. This relatedness leads to worship of God, unavoidably so. We may then determine that humanity is a worshipping species, that worship is a part of our nature. God's early creations before us, the plant and animal life, obviously could not offer this worshipful response to God. Today we can believe we are not alone in an indifferent and hostile universe — that yes, we were made for a loving and meaningful relationship with the Creator, by the Creator.

From the perspective of relationship with God, we might view that without God, we humans would be a lonely people. With God, there can be the experience of wonderful worship, praise and adoration; without God, there can be a feeling of emptiness and sensations of being cut off. Without real relating, the result is dire human loneliness, as if disconnected or "outside, looking in." Loneliness, as many of us know, is a common human problem in our society and elsewhere: loneliness is a problem facing many of us today, perhaps all of us at one time or another.

> You can find lonely people by standing on any street corner in urban America. Scan the faces of the other persons on the curb. Notice the vacant stares, the empty eyes, the expressionless mouths. These are people who look as if they were only half alive. Some of them may be absorbed in their thoughts. But the large majority are just standing there — alone in a crowd and possibly lonely.
>
> Lonely people include the executive on the way up who no longer talks to his wife; the young man or woman alone for the first time in an apartment complex in a large city; the suburban housewife surrounded by small children and by neighbors whom she does not know.[11]

We can consider this problem of loneliness more directly, for a loving and caring God surely would not wish us to be hindered by any incapacitating source. It obviously affects those living apart from others, but also those living in large urban areas — cities where teeming multitudes of people reside. Yes, we want to believe God surely would not have us be lonely, yet loneliness is a fact and a problem to acknowledge. It directly affects our relationships with others and with God, a hindrance to any close abiding relationship. Situations of loneliness touch upon other aspects of life as well,

---

[11] Velma Darbo Stevens, *A Fresh Look at Loneliness* (Nashville: Broadman Press,

such as attitudes regarding priorities and also one's motivation to undertake normal, everyday activities. We can surely assume our loving and caring God would desire for matters of loneliness to be dealt with, as our human health depends on it. Considering that the Creator God was without human beings on earth for apparently a period of many centuries, we can even dare to wonder aloud the strange possibility of God once lonely . . . a God who would then definitely understand our human condition of being disconnected and apart from others. Holy Being God does understand us, in all our human conditions, for we are in God's very image, possessing a real likeness at least in some ways.

Who are the lonely people? One recent writer phrased that question and answered it: "Who are the lonely people? They are not hard to find. They are all around us. In fact, one of them sometimes is living inside your skin. Everyone is lonely at times. Some people are lonely most of the time."[12] Today we realize any list of the lonely may go on still further, to include the traveling salesperson and others who work far from home, such as truck drivers, government employees and military personnel. The large population of college students could also be added to such a list, for they are newly separated from familiar ties of family and old friends. Others who certainly often feel the keen pain of loneliness in their lives would be the single person, whether divorced or never married, and the elderly, many of whom are faced with no alternative but to reside in nursing homes or rest homes. Add to these those people we may rarely come across in our daily routines, such as those in hospitals and prisons. Adolescents and young adults are often lonely individuals, deeply wanting to relate; indeed, they provide a large portion of suicide statistics, mostly due to disconnectedness, despair and little hope. We generally find sharply increased numbers of tragedies and attempted suicides during holidays like Thanksgiving and Christmas, which emphasize family relationships and togetherness in general. It seems loneliness knows no break in holidays. Many shut-ins are also lonely in that their wish to be remembered is usually overlooked by many in their community. From all of these examples we discover that disconnectedness is all around us — a lonely person is probably not far away.

1981), 9.
[12] Stevens, 9.

In our current times we may conclude that the society in which we live might contribute to loneliness for many. It is difficult for many people to maintain identity and meaningful relationships in our increasingly urbanized social environment. It is possible to believe that the places where we live have much to do with this. We can feel as if we are cut adrift upon a sea of humanity — an odd feeling, actually, a combination of being utterly surrounded and yet lonely at the same time. The single person would know full well such oddness as when in the midst of a gathering of married couples — the single, numerically speaking an odd number anyway, oftentimes feels like "a fifth wheel." Being surrounded and yet feeling so lonely is more commonplace than we might first believe.

Attempts to define loneliness can be made having achieved sufficient awareness of its frequent occurrence and nature: it is a painful lack of meaningful and close *relationships* with others, a disjunction or a disconnectedness, maybe even a feeling of being cast asunder. Loneliness leads to an emptiness, melancholy, isolation, or despair. Often a sense of rejection and a low self-image develop whereby one feels an inability to relate, a sense of being left out and possibly unwanted as well. The struggles of the lonely person may embody feeling remote or impertinent as an alien feels rootless or fragmented.

In the answers to the question, "Who are the lonely?" a more typical response given in this society, as in societies before, might have been the example of the widowed person. The widow may be most at peril to the struggles of loneliness. The biblical writer of the Old Testament book of Lamentations chose the lonely widow to personify the city of Jerusalem, a city which suffered great sorrow from destruction at the hands of the Babylonians. The biblical writer presents to us the image of the widowed city, noting the carnage left behind by the conquerors. The literary use of the widow describes the context of the city (from Lamentations 1:1-2):

> How lonely sits the city that was full of people! How like a widow has she become, she that was great among the nations! She that was a princess among the cities has become a vassal. She weeps bitterly in the night, tears on her cheeks; among all her lovers she has none to comfort her; all her friends have dealt treacherously with her, they have become her enemies.

We have now felt the loneliness of an ancient biblical account. We know the widow is vulnerable to the occurrences of disconnectedness, then and now. Perhaps, we too have sensed the same lack of relating ourselves, in the past or in our present. It appears that the infirmity of disconnectedness can reach us all, at least at times; we can recognize ourselves in these lonely words of suffering. Yet, we can rest in confidence in our God through such difficult times that come upon us. Our strength comes from the Eternal God, who might have been lonely before creating humankind ages ago, who will, in the relationship of love and care, be our fortress in our faith. This we not only continue to hope, but rely on. God is our companion; God's spirit can strengthen our human spirit. A prayer for companionship of the spirit is as follows:

> Eternal Father, Thou who art the companion of those who need Thee: Be Thou our companion. Pass with us through the valley of loneliness and stand with us beyond its turmoil. Stir us to find heaven in common things and friendliness in the commonplace. Make us to be friendly. In the weary hours of dark nights and the drudgery of slow turning days, we would remember Thee; when others forget us in their busy routine, Thou wilt not forget. Build Thou within us a new companionship, a companionship of the spirit. As the sea is to the ship, as the air is to the bird, so art Thou unto us in our meditation. So we would know Thee and Thy ways of working for the sake of Jesus. Amen.[13]

Considering the far distant past in our backward glance, we may now accept that the loving and caring Creator God first made all plant life and all animal life, and then later on, created humans in the divine image. The significance is that this act of creating the ultimate awesome creation of life in human beings was not a mere afterthought. God desired our close relationship, wanting us to relate to God, now also just as God did then. God wishes, desires and yearns for our fellowship and love, and for a relationship for an eternity, at that! God offered this to the first human beings, and even today, God offers this to you and me, to all of us.

---

[13] Richard C. Cabot and Russell L. Dicks, *The Art of Minstering to the Sick* (New York: The Macmillan Company, 1936), 226.

CHAPTER 9

MADE IN THE IMAGE OF GOD

What does it mean to say humans are made in the image of God? The final, ultimate answer is this: "we just do not fully know yet what that means. We are still growing spiritually."

First of all, do we really know what God is like? Perhaps, before attempting to develop some answer as to what we ourselves may be like when made in the image of God, we might consider again some aspects of what our God is like. Here lies the main portion of this problem. Possibly, like the apostle Paul's words, we too may only know and see "through a glass darkly." God often seems simply too far beyond human grasp. However, we do have several revealing characteristics of God though made known to us over time — and from none other than God as the source! Even so, what we have received we have seen through human eyes, heard through human ears and interpreted it through human minds. The process has largely seemed to involve God revealing and offering to humankind, with humans on the receiving end.

At the outset we know God is eternal and everlasting. God was God before time and will be God after time is gone. God is the Lord over time — past, present and future are equally vivid to God. God is not trapped, so to speak, in the time stream, though God so loved us as to send Jesus as Christ into our time and space on this earth. Time then does have meaning for God, as God chose when and how to send Christ among us in human form; we must, however, realize that God is eternal and everlasting.

We can also hold that God is both loving and caring, as we remember the often quoted short piece of scripture, "God is love." This is a simple statement, though quite complex in meaning. God loves us even when we do not measure up to divine standards for the proper relationship with others or with God. When we fail, God still loves us. God does not love our sinfulness, our bigotry, our prejudices, our hatred, etc. but God still offers divine love to each of us, a love freely given. As for our transgressions, God offers the divine, all-encompassing forgiveness freely given if only we recognize our wrong, confess and strive to redirect our lives accordingly. Indeed, God is love.

As powerful as these characteristics are, the aspects of being righteous and holy may seem to sharply denote God's otherworldliness. Being completely righteous and holy, God can and does command justice from humankind — surely many have experienced and many will experience the awesome, awfully just hand of God due to their inhumane treatment of others through sheer evil perpetrated on this earth. Yet, closely related to God's just and holy aspects is the mercy extended according to God's own determination. All of us should be immensely thankful, beyond all measure, that our merciful God is our judge. Of course, exactly how the justice/mercy tension really works itself out when an individual is judged is simply and completely within God's domain and control, not ours. God is a righteous God, a holy God — as well as a God of love and mercy.

Other characteristics of God involve elements of infiniteness. This infiniteness is often expressed by most all theologians as omnipotence (all-powerful), omniscience (all-knowing), and omnipresence (all-present). Speaking generally, most Christian theologians agree that omnipotence means that God

can do anything that is consistent with God's own will and nature — that there are no limitations imposed on God from without. God chose limits when the Creator God conceived this world giving the created humans their freedom. Regarding God's omniscient nature, the generally held views would include that God knows all about us; nothing can be hidden from God; God knows future events; and the wisdom and knowledge of God are unfathomable. (An important note which should caution us all: God's foreknowledge does *not* mean pre-determining events, since God gave freedom to humankind.) Then finally, regarding God's infinite qualities, most theologians agree that God is not spatially confined or limited, and that God is inescapable. Since God is spirit, the divine being can be thought of as close to each of us as a person's breathing, and of course poetically, as within one's heart. From the evidence of God's being all-powerful, all-knowing and all-present, the infiniteness of God contrasts sharply with the finite limitations of human beings.

One word which has occurred in the above statements regarding aspects of God's being is "freedom." In God's creator role, God chose to bring life into the world, and set human beings in dominion over this world God created. God did this freely, one must stress — God did not have to bring us into being, but did so out of generous love, and God included freedom for God's created beings. Along with this freedom humankind would have to be responsible with the use of it. We are free to follow God or even to rebel against God — that choice belongs to each of us, individually. Moreover, Eternal God has communicated divine love and freedom to us by sending Christ Jesus directly into our time and space. By that act of sending Christ into our time stream, God further revealed to us much of the nature of God's being that we do know: through the life and ministry of Jesus as Christ came God's offering of love, peace and hope to us all. Further still, we might recall the saying of Jesus, "If you see me, you have seen the Father." So, we might infer that as the revelation of God through Jesus Christ was made through that person and ministry here on earth, Christ provided his followers and disciples a unique and direct insight into the character of God's being.

Having addressed quite briefly what God may be like, we may now consider more specifically how human beings are made in the image of God. First of all, if we regard highly the creator role for God, then it can follow that created beings would be, of course, thought of as creatures, as in that "creative" sense. Quite literally, we are creatures created by the Creator. On one hand, this idea of human creatureliness would seem to place us within the general framework of numerous species of animals which roam and exist on this planet: such a notion has, it would seem, a connotation which tends to drag down human beings below the lofty level where we would wish to be. On the other hand, to be considered a creature created by the Creator might also be interpreted as akin to reflecting the handiwork of the Master Creator artisan, as artists' personal aspects can usually be found in their handiwork. In that sense the human level could appear lofty indeed! Moreover, we should not view ourselves as too lowly for God chose to commune with us — through many prophets of centuries long gone, directly breaking into our time and space by sending Jesus as Christ around 7 BC to 33 AD (in the Palestine/Israel area of the Middle East region of our world), and of course, directly ever since within our souls through the Holy Spirit dimension of God's being. So God has chosen to risk communication with each of us, if only one would listen to the still, small voice within, as it is so often poetically described. In summary, through our Creator God's handiwork of us humans and also God's choosing to commune with us, we may infer some real relatedness with God. All the ingredients of a genuine relationship are present, one could say. Our level of created beings has indeed a lofty place — in relation to God, no less!

Additional views of ourselves might include an idea that we are creators too. The Creator God, in fashioning us provided us with much capacity for intelligence and creativity so that we in turn enjoy fashioning our world, utilizing our freedoms. Over the centuries, technological advances in areas of science, medicine and agriculture are only a few examples of the positive creative ventures human beings have thrust forward within our own world — displaying our own human interest in the creation process. We could be so bold as to point to this creative aspect as the place where we have a similarity with God, though with the acknowledgment of our finiteness compared to God's infiniteness. Nevertheless, we are creators too, even if in much smaller measure.

Another meaningful connection with God's being, one closely related to *God's* choosing to commune with us, is *our* choosing to commune with God through prayers. By our daily human initiatives of desiring to petition God, or to complain to God, to ask for forgiveness from God or to lift up praise or thanksgiving to God's hearing — we are attempting to reach out to God, to connect with the eternal Holy Being. By so doing, we are raising ourselves spiritually to an ever closer level of oneness with God, actually experiencing a loving relationship which offers divine peace and true grace to the soul of the praying follower or seeker. So this last aspect of wishing to commune with God may be further support in establishing for ourselves our human claim of being made in the image of God.

Ideas, however, do exist which appear to counter these claims of God's image within us. These aspects center around contrasting characteristics of our being and God's being. They may seem to be strong evidence of major, stark differences between us and our concept of God. If we accept that God is eternal, everlasting, loving, caring, righteous and holy, then we may discern our utter human disconnectedness in like manner, namely: human beings 1) are not eternal on this earth but temporal beings here for some finite length of time, spanning maybe 80-90 years or so, 2) are loving and caring at times but regrettably failing noticeably often in our love and care to others and even to self also, 3) are not always righteous to be sure, though usually possessing good and even admirable intentions toward others, and 4) obviously not holy, but hopefully growing spiritually toward an ever holier existence, enabling some real peace with oneself, one's God and with those persons one encounters daily. Quite possibly, it is precisely here at this final point which may sound the most hopeful note for our human lot in claiming some essence of the image of God: spiritual growing offers us all access to the real dimension of God's essence and greater movement toward genuine oneness with God — if not holiness, then genuine oneness with God, and then if not right now, maybe someday ahead.

If we are beginning to arrive at a conclusion as to what we can make of our creation in God's image, we can unfortunately discover mounds and mounds of dire examples of our human shortcomings in our history. Nevertheless, we simply cannot overlook numerous instances of goodness in our wondrous seeking for God over our span of years here on earth. By seeking oneness with God during our journey of life we may hope to realize and enjoy the arms of God drawing us in and holding us dear: this we hope, as we recall expressions of hope made before — one's heart is restless until it finds its rest in God.

Any hopeful human grasping for a lofty level near God's being is often quite awkward, difficult and even strewn with risks. One rather remarkable story touching upon the loftiness of our fervent hopes involves the ideal of freedom — a story drawn from the pages of the American era at its beginnings, about the author of this nation's Declaration of Independence in the later part of the eighteenth century. This, the most notable and famous of Thomas Jefferson's accomplishments, was conceptually profound and uniquely fundamental to this nation's birth, in that it touched directly upon the lofty ideals of freedom and liberty. History calls us to remember that no British colonies had ever (to that time) successfully challenged the government of England for actual independence — and the awesome consequences of failure were for the active proponents to be branded as traitors, soon followed by certain death by hanging. Thus, the business of rebelling for freedom was a serious endeavor, not to be taken lightly but with a measured manner and a seriousness of purpose instead. Jefferson's brilliant mind and his ability to summarize national sentiment with eloquence and clarity thrust him up among the great leaders of his time.

> When in the Course of human events, it becomes necessary for one people to dissolve the political bonds which have connected them with another, and to assume among the powers of the earth, the separate and equal station to which the Laws of Nature and of Nature's God entitle them, a decent respect to the opinions of mankind requires that they should declare the causes which impel them to the separation. We hold these truths to be self-evident, that all men are created equal, that they are endowed by their Creator with certain inalienable rights, that among these are Life, Liberty and pursuit of Happiness. That to secure these rights, governments are instituted among men, deriving their just powers from the consent of the governed ....[14]

The document's spirit of freedom, which Jefferson articulated with obvious eloquence, lifted up human ideals soon to be regarded as the founding guideposts of American democracy. The document also brought about much internal debate regarding the rights of all living within the colonial lands: the document's spirit of freedom expressed language specifying the equality of all, thus providing much impetus in his day to address the saddening episode of slave ownership. Yet, one particular development became most striking and noticeable: even the author of these eloquent, moving, liberating ideals still owned slaves at the time of writing the Declaration. Moreover, during the later decades following the American Revolution, when many of his contemporaries (like George Washington and others) and even close neighbors freed their slaves, Thomas Jefferson did not do so.[15] As this country's third president, he chose to remain in his comfortable setting continuing his slave ownership. The very wise crafter of the great and influential freedom document, the document which lifted human

---

[14] Thomas Jefferson, "The Declaration of Independence," *Norton Anthology of American Literature*, ed. Nina Baym, 2nd ed., vol. 1 (New York: Norton, 1985) 610-611.

[15] Kay McFadden, "The Many Faces of Thomas Jefferson," *The Charlotte Observer* 18 Feb. 1997: 1D, 2D.

spirits to lofty levels in fervent hopes of unchaining shackles for genuine liberty, chose himself not to live by that same spirit in his own household.

Today as we briefly review this small bit of our history, we no doubt sense the disturbing tug within our hearts from the obvious contradiction and irony presented. Of course, we of today's society and present culture can easily point out significant human frailties in hindsight, and wince over Thomas Jefferson's puzzling inconsistencies between his publicly avowed ideals and his personal actions. We surely support from our own vantage point of today his words of action, yet grimace at his subsequent lack of action in response to his own words. Such moving, liberating expressions of the ideals of freedom could be said to elevate one's soul closer to God's, but human shortcomings, which we all regrettably manifest in some degree, do tend to speak quite loudly as well . . . and for all to hear.

In returning to some conclusion as to how we are in the image of God, possibly we have to strive to exhaust all efforts to learn from the lessons drawn from all of our past and all of our present. We certainly yearn to determine our true relationship with God now and for our time ahead. But for now, it appears that more reflection on past and present is called for, bringing other disciplines in to bear. We recall the biblical writers added some insight to this matter, though not necessarily resulting in wanted clarity: the apostle Paul spoke for himself, but perhaps for us of today as well when he expressed his seeing "through a glass darkly," in reference to our human relationship with God. Yet, he then pressed on with his spiritual journey seeking God. Here possibly is one lesson for us today: we strive on in our journey too, seeking God. We continue on, continue walking.

What does it mean to be made in the image of God? We just do not fully know yet what that means. We are still growing spiritually.

CHAPTER 10

ANSWERS IN THE LONG TERM

From an ancient Hebrew writing which today we can find in the Old Testament book of Job, there is a centuries-old account of a righteous man who underwent a series of personally devastating losses and suffering. Initially he was quite prosperous and was considered blessed, but his abundance soon left him as disaster came and deprivation followed. His was the struggle of a righteous sufferer who knew days without hope (from Job 7:2-6):

> Like a slave who longs for the shadow, and like a hireling who looks for his wages, so I am allotted months of emptiness, and nights of misery are apportioned to me. When I lie down I say, 'When shall I arise?' But the night is long, and I am full of tossing till the dawn. My flesh is clothed with worms and dirt; my skin hardens, then breaks out afresh. My days are swifter than a weaver's shuttle, and come to their end without hope.

In the pressure of events around us, we know all too well of struggles with personal difficulties and losses. They can occur on our own personal level, such as with a family member or another relative, or maybe a friend, neighbor, co-worker or of course oneself. They also occur in larger scale such as those resulting from natural disasters or the violence of war. Pain, suffering, disease, accidents and shock of loss are all tragedies affecting an individual's well-being in profound ways. The pressure of events can even be such that all possibilities for good in life may seem to be gone altogether. Struggles of great hardship appear in the most ancient of centuries-old writings and in the most up-to-date stories of our lives.

> Crying out to God, pleading, begging.
> An honest, true and genuine human response . . .
> to emptiness, silence and utter absence of God.
> God seems hidden, God seems gone. Where is God?
>
> Crying out to God, pleading, begging.
> Hearing no answer, knowing only stillness,
> the dark night of the soul seems so endless.
> God seems hidden, God seems gone. Where is God?
>
> Crying out to God, pleading, begging.
> God has waited for our cries and pleas.
> God wants the honest, true and genuine responses:
> That's what it means to be a human,
> > and some of how God is God.

In our present era in Western society, in the advanced, industrialized countries primarily, it seems we want immediate gratification and immediate responses to our needs and desires. During our daily routines we come upon numerous instances of timely conveniences. We experience express checkout at stores, drive-thru lanes, ATM bank machines, "1 800" telephone numbers, telephone pagers, "instant checking" accounts, passing lanes and turning lanes on highways, and remote control for instant and immediate control of our entertainment — we are really quite impatient! We are spoiled by our modern, timely conveniences. Today we view our relationship with God through the same eyes that have become acclimated to the spoiled pace of life which we live — we wish for God to respond instantaneously to our remote controls, that is, our prayers. Too often we do not understand why God will not respond now to our immediate needs, desires and longings. Why is it God will not answer my prayers right now?

God is God-of-the-long-term. The biblical writer of the New Testament provides us with the account of Jesus dying on the cross. It is an agonizing account. We are told that to God the Father, Jesus cried out in his horrible, painful anguish as he hung on the wooden cross, "Why have you forsaken me?" (Matthew 27:46-50 and Mark 15:34-37). This question can say a great deal about human suffering. The biblical writers apparently could have easily left out this graphic admission of Jesus in his honest questioning of God's involvement (or lack of it) at his dire crisis. Yet, this account has remained for all to read. As we hear this serious, grave and anguished cry to God, we should also note that the biblical writer does not actually provide any instant answer as such, nothing specific at all really, to Jesus' question. In fact, what immediately follows in that account is that Jesus then cried loudly again and breathed his last. Now, just what do we make of this? Was Jesus' question somehow unimportant or irrelevant? Why did God the Father not respond? Jesus cried loudly again, the writer tells us. That's all.

Upon reflection, we today can resolve not to let the apparent absence of a "present" God destroy our faith or derail us in any way. We must just adapt. We simply must change our perspective to accommodate God. The force of reality always tells us we cannot coerce or force God to be more present or to respond instantly as we would wish: God seems to respond according to God's own timing, to God's own timetable. Therefore, we must adapt to the ways of God, for our very faith, if it is well grounded in reality instead of magical thinking, must rely upon God's ways in our lives. It is imperative that we change our perspective in life to accommodate God — for what choice do we have now in that, anyway? This is also God's relationship with us, as individuals.

Regarding the account of Jesus dying on the cross — to his question, there was apparently no answer from God at that time. Quite possibly, it is important to note the words "at that time," because the idea of God being the everlasting, living God carries with it the belief that God can answer in God's own timing. As God is eternal we can surmise that God's answers could conceivably be quite long in coming! We may, in fact, think an answer will never come to our petitions in prayers: we may even become convinced it will not come at all, as we grow angry and even bitter. Nevertheless, the answer may come, some day, God willing. It seems it is up to God.

We live here on this earth for a short span of time; God on the other hand, is timeless, beyond time. God was God before time was and will be God after time ends — God is eternal. So our faith must adapt to reflect an honest, true and genuine relationship with the living God, no matter how hidden or absent that God seems so very, very often. We are people of the short term; God is God of the long term. In fact, this is our place in this world, our place in time. It is possible we might experience, as did the righteous sufferer Job, days and days without hope; or, we might experience anguished hours of pain, questioning God's presence by crying out as utterly forsaken by God, as accounts say Jesus did on that tortuous cross. Whatever may come in our own individual situations, our crying prayers to God are simply not ignored, unheard or unobserved by the God of love. The Everlasting God responds according to God's own timing. It seems it is up to God.

Chapter 11

Sin and Forgiveness

Relating with others is not easy. Regrettably, we often place barriers which effectively block good personal relationships, as we encounter the reality of our own wrongdoing or of being wronged by another. A relationship then usually spoils to some degree and repercussions occur, possibly spinning out of control. Wrongdoing causes so much pain; we often fail, disappoint and hurt others. Relationships are not easy sometimes.

The subject of wrongdoing may be the most unpleasant of religious topics. (Acts of wrongdoing, for our purposes of discussion, can include sin, crime and evil.) Really, who among us truly wishes to dwell very much on such unpleasant matters? Thankfully, we can combine this element of wrongdoing with the element of forgiveness, as our merciful God allows this. If discussing wrongdoing can be unpleasant, we can find discussing forgiveness to be overwhelmingly wonderful in comparison.

Some general distinctions can be drawn in human acts of wrongdoing, as different terms will project varying images depending on their context. 1) First of all, the word "sin" tends to be used as a religious term. 2) The word "crime" is used by lawyers and law enforcement sectors of society. 3) The word "evil" is most commonly preferred by philosophers, used in general conceptual ways. The difference in these terms for our use in relationship issues may be best seen by way of the biblical account stating, "All have sinned and fallen short of the glory of God" — whereas very few of us, hopefully, have participated in crime or engaged in evil, though these terms can obviously overlap in meaning. But for the religious use in dealing with relationships and how barriers are often placed in the way of good healthy relating, the term "sin" seems to involve aspects of the human condition of us all: we all may seem often to fail, disappoint and hurt others.

Biblical sources offer that we all have sinned, or missed the mark, in our relationships either by word or action resulting in hurting someone else. Of course, we readily recall instances where someone has hurt us, wronged us and caused hurt feelings and resentment. Unfortunately, there are also many such instances of our own making where we said something we should not have or done something we should not have which harmed someone or damaged the integrity of a relationship. There may be some painful instances which we cannot readily remember as they were so intensely bothersome or disturbing that we buried them deep in our minds so as not to dwell on the ugliness of that sin; obviously we would much prefer considering ourselves rather highly and above such wrongdoing. We all surely, and almost always, possess good intentions toward others, or the best of intentions, we might say.

With our sins we disappoint others. Because of our sinfulness, we have even hurt others and at least set back relationships — acts which require mending later on in order to renew our communion. Unfortunately, the consequences of our words or deeds may be serious and long-lasting. We may also attempt to shift responsibility of our wrongdoing elsewhere, to a third party or even to that person wronged — though we really cannot forever avoid and evade personal responsibility and owning up to wrongs we have committed.

With our sins we disappoint God. Because of our sinfulness, we have even hurt God. God loves us; God loves us all, so we can very easily believe God is disappointed in our sin as a loving parent is hurt by the wrongs of a child. Of course, God does not love our sins or our sinfulness, but God continues to love us all — yes, even as sinners. We must admit that through sin we not only disappoint others around us, but we do in fact disappoint our God. There is general support for this view of sin within the Christian circles of theologians, based largely upon scriptural understanding: "Sin is basically an offense against God. Although by sinning people cannot do God any actual harm, they do act against God, by despising him and his commandments, and by injuring others (or themselves), since the person injured is also an object of divine providence and protection."[16] And again:

---

[16] Leopold Sabourin, S.J., "Sin," *The Oxford Companion to the Bible*, eds. Bruce M.

"As it is God who is the norm and reason for man's rightness, so it is God against whom every sin is an attack, to whom every sin is an affront. This is not to say, of course, that no others are hurt by the sin, one's self indeed most damaged of all. It is to say that whatever the harm to neighbor or self, it is God who suffers most of all and always."[17]

The ancient voices of the biblical psalmists offer us of today memorable and moving statements expressing much of the sinner's relationship with God. Psalm 51 supplies us with images displaying the human need for God's cleansing of sin and the need for God's presence to restore the relationship (verses 1-15):

> Have mercy on me, O God,
> according to your steadfast love;
> according to your abundant mercy
> blot out my transgressions.
> Wash me thoroughly from my iniquity,
> and cleanse me from my sin.
> For I know my transgressions,
> and my sin is ever before me.
> Against you, you alone, have I sinned,
> and done what is evil in your sight,
> so that you are justified in your sentence
> and blameless when you pass judgment.
> Indeed, I was born guilty,
> a sinner when my mother conceived me.
>
> You desire truth in the inward being;
> therefore teach me wisdom in my secret heart.
> Purge me with hyssop, and I shall be clean;
> wash me, and I shall be whiter than snow.
> Let me hear joy and gladness;
> let the bones that you have crushed rejoice.

Metzger and Michael D. Coogan (New York: Oxford University Press, 1993) 696.

[17] John I Durham, "Psalms," *The Broadman Bible Commentary*, ed. Clifton J. Allen,

> Hide your face from my sins,
> and blot out all my iniquities.
>
> Create in me a clean heart, O God,
> and put a new and right spirit within me.
> Do not cast me away from your presence,
> and do not take your holy spirit from me.
> Restore to me the joy of your salvation,
> and sustain in me a willing spirit.
>
> Then I will teach transgressors your ways,
> and sinners will return to you.
> Deliver me from bloodshed, O God,
> O God of my salvation,
> and my tongue will sing aloud of your deliverance.
>
> O Lord, open my lips,
> and my mouth will declare your praise.

Regarding the sinner, God offers real forgiveness, "a clean heart," if one truly is sorry, remorseful, regretting the hurt that was caused to the other person and to God. Recognizing another's pain caused by the sin, whether it is one's neighbor, someone at work, one's family member, or some person whose name is not even known, if the sinner really regrets that sinful act and pleads forgiveness from the Holy God the sins will be forgiven completely. To the sinner, Christ said, "Thy sins are forgiven, go and sin no more." God offers this relief to each of us as a saving, grace-ful offer if only we ask for it and accept it. One might sense the weight of the world suddenly lifted from the shoulders as genuine peace sets in: "Peace I leave with you" were words often attributed to Christ.

God believed in us, and in our potential as human beings when the Creator God made us in the Creator's image. Even after humankind sinned so grievously over many centuries, God sent Christ into the world, into our time and place here on earth. Did God have to do that? It would seem that God

---

vol. 4 (Nashville: Broadman Press, 1971) 275-276.

certainly did not have to provide for us and to us the ministry and person of Jesus Christ. For God so loved us all that God sent Jesus as Christ so that whoever would believe his message of hope and saving grace would not know spiritual death from sinful wrongdoing, but everlasting life, as one's spirit lives on eternally in God's presence. Christian belief holds that after bodily death kindred spirits of faithful followers join with the Creator's spirit in what must certainly be an absolutely marvelous and wondrous event to behold — when those barriers to a personal relationship with God are obviously and completely gone forever.

It is possible to consider the barriers to personal relationships as actually tied to the barriers in our relationships with God. The scriptural accounts provide several instances which we can point to as connecting these relationships — by experiencing the gracious manner in which God forgives us our wrongs, we may then understand a way to let go of our resentments of others' wrongdoings against us. The references in the New Testament of the Lord's Prayer, for example (Matthew 6:12), show that the petition for God's forgiveness is closely linked with our acts of forgiveness to one another here on earth ("forgive us our debts, as we also have forgiven our debtors"). There is a further linkage provided (in the following verses, 14-15) for our guidance in relationships: "For if you forgive others their trespasses, your heavenly Father will also forgive you; but if you do not forgive others, neither will your Father forgive your trespasses."

These guiding principles may sound like stark warnings or a tough message to us all, yet they may convince us that a forgiving spirit in our hearts can place us in the right stead not only in the relationships around us but also before the approving eyes of God. God surely requires us to "let go" of others' wrongs against us since we would obviously wish for others to "let go" of the wrongs we have committed against them. To be perfectly candid now, we must admit that it can be extremely difficult to forgive someone who has really hurt or betrayed us, by betraying our trust for example, maybe wronging us irreversibly. It might feel completely impossible to forgive that person, for the emotions swirling inside are so real and great as if to burst forth with rage directed at that person (all the while convinced it to be entirely justified). The emotion may strengthen our conviction and we can ask ourselves, "How can I ever forgive and forget that wrong done against me by that person?" Also, it is so easy to be completely swayed that such a terrible wrong deserves swift punishment as well. An answer right here to "How can one forgive?" will address this — and the answer will indeed come, from our Holy, Righteous, Just (and Merciful) God, no less; maybe not right away or as soon as we would like to receive it, but it will indeed come in time. (In the case of a truly horrible violent criminal act, the answer may not come at all in the short term, but may take years, and then also a lot of time to overcome such a devastating wrongdoing.) This has always been tremendously difficult to accept, and may continue to be this way. For our emotional, mental and spiritual well-being, we need to keep in focus that biblical statement linking our acts of forgiving others to God's acts of forgiving us. God seems to link them. Such connections here are unavoidable: like it or not, our relationships here on this earth are linked to our individual relationships with Eternal God.

There are other essential elements of forgiveness which God appears to require of us to understand. There is nothing automatic about forgiveness, and forgiveness is received only by one actually willing to change and turn away from that sin.[18] Merely requesting God or someone in a personal relationship to forgive a particular wrongdoing and then promptly resuming the sinful behavior, as in some set pattern of actions, hardly convinces the forgiving party that our stated confessions and intentions merit the gift of forgiveness. Genuine forgiveness can only be available to those who are really willing to change old attitudes regarding the wrongdoing and then desire to get rid of the sin altogether to restore the relationship. We recall the ancient words of the psalmist, "Create in me a clean heart, O God, and put a new and right spirit within me." Forgiveness requires more than mere requesting of it; the admission may in fact be rather painful to express and then the resulting changes required will demand radically different behavior, an actual turning from the old ways to acquire "a new and right spirit." It may be quite costly to be so reminded of our dependence upon God and acknowledgment of being wrong, as our pride may suffer. Reconciliation requires much of us. Reliable and healthy relationships, though, with God and with others, are so valuable in our lives as to warrant the high costs of repair. Forgiveness enhances our relationships, opening the doors to a richer life in our future, if that barrier of sin is removed and appropriately resolved. When we can be kind to one

---

[18] David Atkinson, "Forgiveness," *Eerdman's Handbook to Christian Belief*, ed. Robin Keeley (Grand Rapids: Wm. B. Eerdman's Publishing Co., 1982), 290.

another, tenderhearted, and forgive one another as God forgives us, relationships can develop further, offering to us the added benefits or fruits of good health. "Restore to me the joy of your salvation, and sustain in me a willing spirit . . . O Lord, open my lips, and my mouth will declare your praise.

Chapter 12

Bad Relating / Prejudice

A common vice in our society and culture today which is blatantly wrong and hurtful to others is prejudice. Prejudice can be defined as stereotyping emotional reactions that predispose one to consistently react in a negative way toward a given class of persons. This is a well-rooted problem today and has surely been around since ancient days, probably since people first have been unable to get along, in one sense or another. In a biblical reference from the New Testament we find a classic example of ethnic or class prejudice. The biblical writer has Jesus' response to a question posed by a lawyer. Their conversation dealt with relationships as Jesus stressed the importance of loving one's neighbor as oneself (from Luke 10:29-37).

> But wanting to justify himself, he asked Jesus, "And who is my neighbor?" Jesus replied, "A man was going down from Jerusalem to Jericho, and fell into the hands of robbers, who stripped him, beat him, and went away, leaving him half dead. Now by chance a priest was going down that road; and when he saw him, he passed by on the other side. So likewise a Levite, when he came to the place and saw him, passed by on the other side. But a Samaritan while traveling came near him; and when he saw him, he was moved with pity. He went to him and bandaged his wounds, having poured oil and wine on them. Then he put him on his own animal, brought him to an inn, and took care of him. The next day he took out two denarii, gave them to the innkeeper, and said, 'Take care of him; and when I come back, I will repay you whatever more you spend.' Which of these three, do you think, was a neighbor to the man who fell into the hands of the robbers?" He said, "The one who showed him mercy." Jesus said to him, "Go and do likewise."

As that story unfolds, we learn that the priest could not stop and aid the victim. The reasons often cited by biblical scholars include two: 1) for all the priest knew, the unconscious man might have been dead, and religious law held that to touch the body (to determine if he was alive) would have defiled the priest — so the pious priest could not help this person, 2) there was no way to determine who this naked and beaten man really was, as there was no means of identification possible due to the situation. The man was obviously a human being who became a helpless victim of evil by robbers — one at the wrong place at the wrong time, we tend to say. Yet, the man was also the victim secondly by a high member of the religious clergy, a priest — for the accepted mode of thought of that day regarding neighbors defined a neighbor as one very much like yourself, not someone of a different class or ethnic group. So, the inference was that a "real" neighbor could indeed be aided, but since this person might not be a neighbor, then obviously the best thing to do was simply to pass by as far from him as possible. Jesus then adds the second traveler; but being a Levite, a helper to the priests in the Temple, the response to the victim was the same and probably for the same reasons. Then Jesus adds the third traveler, a Samaritan, to happen by the victim (a Samaritan, of all people! Samaritans and Jews held much prejudice for each other). Yet, it would be this third traveler, of all people, who would be the helpful neighbor to the person in dire need. Jesus set the accepted mode of thought of that day and culture upside down with his story. Had Jesus responded to the question of "Who is my neighbor?" with the direct, simple answer of "everyone," the effect would not have been the same as the long story he offered. We can notice that Jesus offers more than the answer given: he also instructed the lawyer to go and show mercy on others as was the reaction of the Samaritan in the story. Certainly, this was more of an answer than the lawyer expected or really wanted to hear — people rarely like to have their prejudices pointed out to them. We today do not either.

Prejudice appears to be around us all, everywhere we go. The prejudiced individual over-generalizes from past experience and rigidly holds onto preconceptions. By doing this the misconception can become, in effect, irreversible. Racial prejudice, we should note, is generally marked by the individual's desire to avoid, malign or express hostilities toward an ethnic group of people. Resulting actions range from maintaining social distance, to discrimination and to various forms of hostility and aggression. Other behavioral actions often include ethnic jokes and slurs, either directed at someone personally or privately within one's circle of friends. Unfortunately, so much, though not all, of this "acceptable" behavior and attitude tends to be passed on from generation to generation by parents and family. Surely we know society as a whole pays a dear price for the hurtful actions of a small group of individuals, reinforcing rigid misconceptions within their minds with jokes and slurs that put others down. It would seem healthy family values taught within the family unit should stress peace and love toward others who we would not ordinarily consider our neighbors or family.

Another side of prejudice common in society is that known as religious intolerance. Our holding different religious faiths has historically divided the human family into many groups, separate from one another. Quite often the different groups have very little to do with each other. Regrettably all too often, faiths containing differing perspectives regarding God and religious practices have become quickly maligned as somehow unworthy even to be tolerated. Worse still, many instances of religious persecution has also occurred in history whereby one group, with political and/or military strengths over others, takes advantages, forcibly dominates, or even pushes out others deemed harmful or seen as rivals. This still happens today as well. Quite common presently is the more subtle separations. Yes, people with other faiths are often considered far too different from ourselves to be deemed acceptable in our mindset. So it is precisely here at the human mindset where we can directly focus upon: we humans just have to think differently, being more open-minded. The world today is a smaller place due to advanced means of communication, allowing us to be much more aware of other faiths' existence. Many, if not most, groups of our fellow humankind are actually along a similar journey of personal faith. Allowing the gentle prompting of the Divine voice within, our minds can indeed be more open and accepting to consider that even though there are divergent belief patterns existing within the human family, there really is a universal seeking after the Divine essence. This book, although primarily holding to the Christian traditions, would be amiss to leave out the contention that the array of world religions probably have more in common with each other than differences, especially in regard to an individual's relationship with God. Hopefully, all of us, as equal children of God, can allow without necessarily agreeing, a respect of others' beliefs. Most of us surely have common ideals for individual relating in peace and love. Within those common ideals we all have the right to believe differently as some aspects of religious matters prompt a differing emphasis and priority. Certainly we can believe that God would have us all diligently strive to continue on our journey of faith, without denying others their interpretation of religious beliefs. Creator God fashioned us, everyone, as free beings, and free to choose to love God in our own individual manner.

Elie Wiesel, perhaps the most prominent spokesperson for the survivors of the Holocaust, has pointed out on numerous occasions his reflections and thoughts of the World War II tragedy and of surviving the fury's aftermath. He was growing up in northern Romania when Germany's ruling Nazis swept through and then swept him and his family into the Auschwitz and Buchenwald concentration camps, the final places for Jews and others considered inferior by the Nazis. His parents and a sister were murdered there. The numbers of the murdered victims of that Holocaust are so difficult to fathom: all told, it is estimated some 6,000,000 Jews and 5,000,000 others fell to the Nazis. Those numbers of lives snuffed out sound horrific, almost too horrible to believe. Yet, they were indeed swept away by a terrible holocaust, one still remembered by many, including elderly survivors of the horrors. "It is very deep in the memory of humanity. Whether it knows it or not . . . the winds of madness were blowing."[19]

In addressing that past madness, Wiesel has stressed fanaticism to be the world's worst enemy, with indifference being a close second. "We must be involved in other people's affairs. We can't say, 'Why should I care about something I can't do anything about?' That is the first step to indifference. If you feel indifferent to their plight, you will feel indifferent to people you see on your own street."[20]

With the great personal loss which he experienced from that madness, Wiesel has even dared to address his being angry with God. "I still am, but always from inside faith, not outside faith. . . . In my religion (Judaism), we are allowed to do so. . . . Even today at times, I do question God's ways." Admitting his anger, he has stated he is not bitter, though the Holocaust robbed him of his faith in humanity — but only to a point. "What's the

---

[19] Ken Garfield, "'Teach One Person'," *The Charlotte Observer* 13 March 1997: 1A, 15A.
[20] Garfield 15A.

alternative? We must become more optimistic. We have no choice but to invest more hope where there is none."[21]

If we of today can return to the ancient story of Jesus and his question of who in fact was the neighbor to the beaten and robbed victim, we need to remember that the answer was not only "the one who showed mercy" but also "go and do likewise." To the more recent story of the Holocaust, we might now admit we need to remember Elie Wiesel's reflections, "We must be involved in other people's affairs. We can't say, 'Why should I care about something I can't do anything about?' That is the first step to indifference."

To all such stories far away or right here with us, we surely need to remember some answers. Certainly the realization hits home that prejudice is simply wrong and hurtful to others. We know hatred and violence can stem from prejudice, and regrettably, prejudice is all around us. We must not forget.

---

[21] Garfield 15A.

CHAPTER 13

RELATING TO GOD

One's relationship with the Creator God is truly the ultimate relationship one will ever have. It is far more loving, complicated, involved and intimate than any other relationship and covers one's whole lifespan here on earth. Since the Creator God also knew one's parents and grandparents and, of course, beyond them all the way back to creation itself, it is easy to conclude God knows quite well what an individual is all about and "what makes one tick." Then, one can add to this, the fact that surely God continues to know an individual after the person has died in the bodily human form, moving on to the spiritual form to be with God eternally thereafter. So we might indeed conclude one's relationship with the Creator God is in fact the most ultimate relationship one will ever have, surpassing all others.

As with any relationship involving a human being, there may always seem to be "ups and downs." Even with the holy, righteous, loving and caring God, it often appears that an individual's relationship with God is at times an uneasy or even difficult or strained one. To pretend the "downs" do not exist, insisting that all is well all the time, would be to deny the genuine, or real, character of relating to another being, in this case even the Holy Being, God. Ups and downs do happen and of course the difficult times of relating need to be dealt with and worked through, as with any other human relationship here on earth. A relationship that hides troubling issues or uneasy times would be an artificial, or pretend, relationship. One cannot hide difficult matters from one's relationship with God any more than one can hide physically from God. An individual, therefore, might as well be completely candid, open, honest and direct, holding back nothing at all.

The ancient biblical writers of the Psalms in the Old Testament knew of distressing relationships with God themselves. Writers spoke of lamenting to God in quite emotional ways. Actually, psalms of lament are the second most in number of all the types of psalms, second only to the psalms of praise. Lamenting prayers contained obvious stress and trials of the speaker's relationship with God; usually the context was clearly one of spiritual, mental, physical and material suffering. In addition, the psalmist writer was obviously quite candid, honest and direct with feelings openly expressed to God — nothing artificial at all in that relationship. Specifically, the initial cry for a hearing usually included an expression of certainty that God would hear. One psalm, Psalm 88, differs from the others in that it expresses no hope and confesses no faith as such — except that it is, after all, a prayer. A person completely and totally without hope and a sustaining faith would not even bother to pray to God for help. By the very act of prayer itself, one implies at least something in the way of seeking help and hope.

> O LORD, God of my salvation, when, at
> night, I cry out in your presence,
> let my prayer come before you;
> incline your ear to my cry.
>
> For my soul is full of troubles, and
> my life draws near to Sheol.
> I am counted among those who go down
> to the Pit;
> I am like those who have no help,
> like those forsaken among the dead,
> like the slain that lie in the grave,
> like those whom you remember no more,
> for they are cut off from your hand.
> You have put me in the depths of the Pit,
> in the regions dark and deep.
> Your wrath lies heavy upon me, and you
> overwhelm me with all your waves.

You have caused my companions to shun me;
you have made me a thing of horror to them.
I am shut in so that I cannot escape;
my eye grows dim through sorrow.
Every day I call on you, O LORD;
I spread out my hands to you.
Do you work wonders for the dead?
Do the shades rise up to praise you?
Is your steadfast love declared in the grave,
or your faithfulness in Abaddon?
Are your wonders known in the darkness,
or your saving help in the land of forgetfulness?

But I, O LORD, cry out to you;
in the morning my prayer comes before you.
O LORD, why do you cast me off?
Why do you hide your face from me?
Wretched and close to death from my youth up,
I suffer your terrors; I am desperate.
Your wrath has swept over me;
your dread assaults destroy me.
They surround me like a flood all day long;
from all sides they close in on me.
You have caused friend and neighbor to shun me;
my companions are in darkness.

This psalm is a stark cry of human agony. The speaker has suffered long, and without any relief, and quite obviously feels cut off from God as well as cut off from all others. This prayer of lament is seemingly one long desperate cry, showing no real change of direction in theme or personal mood. This person's petition is more than justified, it would appear, as one's very existence is at great peril, and this person cannot see any meaningful existence whatsoever beyond this life. All of life is lonely, stark and anguished. So terrible is its imagery, we might find it painful to read. The near-total blackness of its misery seemingly reflects an honest portrayal of a strained relationship in the context of dire suffering.

The anguish is real, the pain is real, the suffering is real. Only someone who has also felt such depths of similar, genuine suffering would actually know something of this writer's situation. Should someone, even with good intentions, respond, "I know how you feel," who actually never had any such genuine experience in that same depth of pain, the sufferer may instantly detect such falsehood and resent and reject any further attempts of aid from the comforter. Someone wishing to comfort another may be of most help by simply being present, giving time, and actually listening — being present may offer the best ministry to another's dire anguish. To give of one's time to be alongside a sufferer and freely offering to really listen (instead of giving advice) may indeed prove to be the most wonderful gift of care a person can receive.

We can even further wonder if that is precisely what God does oftentimes with our human prayers, our crying out in desperate pleas for help — maybe the very best comfort the loving, caring God may offer is true attention to our cries, a quiet listening. Can we imagine somehow, or attempt to fathom, what it would be like for God to hear over the many centuries vast billions of candid, anguished cries of lament from truly suffering human beings? God would surely be absolutely grieved far beyond any human concept or remote understanding of that holy, divine ministry. What a wondrously attentive and personal God, our Creator God — who so intimately knows of God's countless children in such pain! God does indeed know us, and God definitely hears us. The Creator God, of course, created us in the first place, so our relationship with God is real and genuine. But we may need to remember sometimes that any genuine relationship is two-way — a relationship with God is available to each and every one of us, if only we respond toward God, making our best efforts. It might be noteworthy to point out that the very next psalm in sequence, Psalm 89, begins with these words (verses 1-2).

> I will sing of your steadfast love,
> O LORD, forever;
> with my mouth I will proclaim your
> faithfulness to all generations.
> I declare that your steadfast love is
> established forever;
> your faithfulness is as firm as the heavens.

Chapter 14

God's Presence

Pain, suffering and sorrow:
Existing now . . . these abound.
Spiritual depression is inward found.
We worry, we fear . . . our common reactions.
Eternal God speaks:
> "Do not fear, for I am with you,
> do not be afraid, for I am your God;
> I will strengthen you, I will help you,
> I will uphold you with my victorious
> right hand."

Pain, suffering and struggle:
Existing now . . . these abound.
Spiritual uplifting is inward found.
To worry, to fear . . . unproductive actions.
Apostle Paul speaks:
> "We are afflicted in every way, but not crushed;
> perplexed, but not driven to despair;
> persecuted, but not forsaken;
> struck down, but not destroyed."

Praise, prayer and worship:
Existing now . . . these abound.
My God's presence is inward found.

No worry, no fear . . . love, joy and peace happen.
I can speak:
> "Even though I walk through the darkest valley,
> I fear no evil;
> for you are with me; your rod and
> your staff — they comfort me."

(Based on Isaiah 41:10, II Corinthians 4:8-9, Psalm 23:4.)

CHAPTER 15

GOD AND OUR RESTLESS SPIRIT

We human beings are well aware of the component of time in our lives. Each day we take note of it, plan with it and use it wisely, and sometimes unwisely. Often we take it for granted in that its presence, in a manner of speaking, is with us constantly as we live and work in our busy, fast-paced world. This "natural" element of time, though, is a very mysterious part of our daily human lives; it is obviously a constant earthly companion wherever we are, and herein lies its mystery. We can easily conclude that time is unmistakably an integral and necessary component of our living — "time is of the essence," we might say, and do say. Yet, with all our human involvement with and attention to time, we can be unavoidably baffled as to its inherent element of mystery. We sometimes feel that even the most basic aspects of time confound us uncomfortably.

One such puzzling feature of time pertains to its very nature: do we really even today have any kind of satisfactory answer to that worn-out question of ours, "What time is it?" We ask it or wonder it all the time: we need the watch, clock and calendar to refer to. Whether what follows this question is a specific objective answer of numbers or a general answer more subjective, the question actually presents us with time's elusive mystery — no reliably, suitable answer is available to us, not really. Regarding the question, "What time is it?" a *specific* answer would be the *point in time* as shown on a watch or clock; however, we can soon realize even this presents natural problems. An example could be where one is presently standing in North America — that person's specific time would be several hours off and apart from the time of someone standing at the same, exact, precise instant in Europe or Asia. In fact, the time may even be a day off, as night is on one side of our planet while day is on the other side at any same exact moment. A *general* answer may also be equally difficult because the *place in time* may be quite different for different persons. One example could be where two individuals are asked the simple question, "What time is it?" — one is young, either in the teens or twenties, whereas the other is in the seventies or eighties. We can naturally assume that their subjective answers might vary according to their perspectives of how much lifespan might be left to that individual. The younger could easily feel time is a rather open-ended commodity with a wide array of possibilities still available, whereas the older might very well respond the contrary, feeling few options left. Their perspectives would be generations apart based on their different contexts in life: early-in-life vs. late-in-life. In essence, their differing general answers convey the idea that time is relative.

So, what then of that worn-out question? Its answer apparently depends upon, and varies with, who is being asked. The simple question can result in differing responses, pointing us to the complicated nature of our world and time in which we live. That line or stream of time can be different for us all as it is relative. How it can be so difficult to pin down is largely the stuff of its mystery.

Time is also a mystery in that we have little control of it. Many of us appear frustrated with time management, or actually with the lack of it. Time is elusive for us. Obviously, we realize in our daily living that we cannot see time, cannot hold it, cannot stop it, cannot buy or sell it and oftentimes feel we are running out of it as there is not enough of it left for our specific purposes or activities. Of course to those who relate they "have time on their hands," meaning little to do, concerted efforts to find absorbing hobbies or new interests will quickly fill the void and fight their possible boredom and idleness, offering new vitality to daily life. Generally speaking, most of us in the human race may experience our fast-paced world with different perspectives than do idle persons. The common observation can quickly turn into the complaint, "There is not enough time to do all that needs to be done." Unfortunately, our experiences tend to mirror the fact that we race to complete most tasks, hoping to satisfactorily finish up "in time." There is so little control of time, no real control at all. In our modern age such is our dilemma that we can feel we are sentenced to repeated questions (whether aloud or to oneself) of "What time is it?"

The modern-age version of our plight could be that we are obsessed by our relationship with time. We know that rapid changes, in technology in general and in communication specifically, have transformed our means of dealing with time, as our parents and grandparents speak of time as moving at a slower pace in their day (technological advances were seemingly much further apart back then, their reasoning would be). We feel that we struggle to keep pace with the changes before us. But no matter what perspective we today possess toward time, such as the inevitable notions of it flying away and not having enough, there is one undeniable fact we tend to lose sight of: all persons in the past who have accomplished truly great achievements, remarkable contributions and notable deeds, had in their lives the same amount of time as we do today in our lives. We forget they had the same number of hours in a day, twenty-four, as we possess in our present day — no more and no less, but the same. Our universe was designed just that way. With the realization that great people did somehow, someway, find the time to accomplish much (everything that was accomplished), perhaps we can resolve to follow them. Believing that it is our time now, our turn, possibly we can begin with the basis that we have the same amount of time as did they — and therefore the same real opportunities to accomplish many things, regardless of the hectic pace we usually feel. Maybe this realization will take some of the mystery out of the element of time in our daily living. Yes, God really gives us all the same number of minutes in a day as was given humankind of yesteryear: our knowledge in science should, naturally, convince us of this quite readily, appearances notwithstanding.

The renowned contemporary physicist, cosmologist and Nobel Prize winner Stephen Hawking has spent virtually all of his career in the study of physics with a focus upon the mystery of time. Hawking once stated that for all the past efforts of brilliant scientists, occupied with the development of new theories that seek to provide the long-sought-after complete, workable description of what the universe is (such as in originating with the so-called Big Bang theory of exploding force starting the process of forming the stars, planets and all life), that the matter of *why* was left to others to answer. Scientists concern themselves with the mathematical and the technical primarily. Perhaps the realization is now settling in regarding the religious side of the equation requiring more attention — we can point out that Einstein once asked the question, "How much choice did God have in constructing the universe?" Whatever specific, complete, unified theory of the universe Hawking and other scientists of the cosmos finally arrive at will directly impact such questions as that of Einstein. Their explanation will have profound implications for the role of God as Creator, or initiator of it all. Probably like most scientists, it would seem that physicists' use of the tools of mathematics soon forced their realization that fields of science, the technical side of events, also connect unavoidably with that of religion, or the more subjective, spiritual side of events. In his concluding paragraph of his book, *A Brief History of Time*, Hawking states the following, in part:

> . . . if we do discover a complete theory, it should in time be understandable in broad principle by everyone, not just a few scientists. Then we shall all . . . be able to take part in the discussion of the question of why it is that we and the universe exist. If we find the answer to that, it would be the ultimate triumph of human reason — for then we would know the mind of God.[22]

Possibly some of us can believe humanity will soon possess that thorough understanding of the "why" of the universe's existence. Yet, we may contend that when and how on this earth we will arrive at the point of knowing the mind of God is really uncertain at best, and conceivably out of human reach by God's design. Understanding completely the matters of time with all its mystery has always been elusive. "Some have found help in C.S. Lewis's picture of time as a straight line along which we travel and of God as the whole page on which the line is drawn. God from above or outside or all around contains the whole of time and sees it all. (However) no human analogy or picture can fully explain the mystery of time and eternity."[23] Our human journey in time has allowed much provision for numerous events of fascinating discovery, our learning about the world in which we live. Yet, in all the centuries of time given to us human beings we have struggled greatly to know all about God.

Augustine, perhaps the most influential early church leader from around the fourth century, wrote about the earthly mysteries of the world and the divine world of God. His influence has been deemed profound: many have credited him with developing ideas that fundamentally shaped Christian

---

[22] Stephen W. Hawking, *A Brief History of Time* (New York: Bantam, 1988) 174-175.
[23] Bruce Nicholls, "Time and Eternity," *Eerdman's Handbook to Christian Belief*, ed.

thinking in the Western church formation of theology. Some of his religious views include the following: God is simply not a material Being, but rather a spirit unconfined by limitations of time and space. God is unlimited in time. With all the inherent mystery of awesome cosmic beginnings, the Creator God, in fact, created time and space, all stars and planets of the universe. Actually our notion of time is bound up with the motion of the stars and planets created by the Creator. All the physical objects of the universe and our earthly world, the various diverse plant life and animal life, served as a stage for God's development of our human spirit for our journey through this earthly life. Humankind's spiritual quest for *relationship* with God, more than mere *knowledge* about God, has impelled human beings to continue to seek God, finding God with the heart, in addition to the mind. The church leader Augustine penned the following, "Our hearts are restless until they find their rest in Thee."

It was in this context that Augustine viewed the human spirit as a pilgrim on earth and a citizen of heaven. This human spirit, as a pilgrim here, is a pupil for the time being — learning from all things material of what Creator God has created here for our learning development. When this state of our education is over, upon our death in the human physical body form, our human spirit moves on to the next stage, which is together with Eternal God.[24] All we can really know now of the mysterious nature of existence in our heavenly future is that we will be there in the spirit form and with God who is and has always been spirit.

We humans appear to be fascinated by the mystery of time, as we accept that our own human journey is "measured" in a "lifetime" here on earth. Time is surely controlled by, and subject to, the Creator God who formed time and space. Time is really an artificial way of understanding the duration between what we refer to as the past, through our present and into our future. We actually live in the very mystery of time since we exist in the only real time, the present, but are concerned so much with the past and the future. Past can be thought of as our present memory of yesterdays, other times; what we refer

---

Robin Keeley (Grand Rapids: Wm. B. Eerdman's Publishing Co., 1982), 154.

[24] Henry Thomas and Dana Lee Thomas, "The Pilgrimage of Augustine: From Sinner to Saint," *Our Wonderful World*, eds. Leonard Davidow and Sanford Cobb, vol. 12 (Chicago: Spencer Press, 1956) 364-365.

to as future is our present-moment expectation of tomorrows ahead.[25] So, we can safely say we know just enough of this mystery God created to be utterly awestruck. God, who is unlimited in time and whose realm is eternity, is timeless and not bound by this very system God created. On the other hand, we humans presently are bound by the past, present and future.

Our human journey depends upon the system of mysteries in which we live. The spirit within us all has always seemed mysterious. Yes, our human spirit is confined temporarily in the earthly physical body. But, the human spirit, upon the physical body's death, is then unbound to join with the spirit of God in God's domain of spiritual abode, in what is generally referred to as Heaven. There we will certainly be freed from bodily constraints, to be at one with God — a relationship ever wondrously renewed, probably as comforting as a created being held lovingly by the Creator's arms. Our human curious wondering at God's great mysteries is presently with us, but by then the mystery of time and all else will be gone. Our relationship with our God continues on eternally. "God is the living God, whose presence holds forth the promise of the ever-new. So the declining capacities and falling opportunities of earthly life are replaced by their opposite: a growing crescendo of glory.
 . . . Eternity will not exhaust the constantly expanding wonder of exploring God."[26]

---

[25] Peter M. J. Stravinskas, ed., *Catholic Encyclopedia* (Huntington: Our Sunday Visitor, 1991) 934.

[26] Anthony Thiselton, "Destiny," *Eerdman's Handbook to Christian Belief*, ed. Robin Keeley (Grand Rapids: Wm. B. Eerdman's Publishing Co., 1982), 423.

CHAPTER 16

MAGICAL THINKING OF PRAYERS

Growing up one is from the earliest age exposed to the cultural and societal phenomenon of Santa Claus. A child quickly learns to associate the Christmas holiday season with the wonderful figure known as Santa. Each year as the calendar pages turn closer and closer to the month of December, the Christmas season enters our daily thoughts. As the vast commercialism of retail business gears up its advertising lures and works at enticing buyers to purchase specific products as presents, for others or ourselves, a child's mind focuses on a list of wants for Christmas. Most all of us know that traditionally such a list typically would include some wonderful items, usually toys but certainly not limited to them: the list is of items most desired because of the pleasure which they would bring the child. Naturally the child's mind would be filled with great anticipation since giving this list to Santa would bring about an overwhelming expectation of receiving all those items on Christmas morning, if one was deemed good during the year. Whatever was defined as good behavior would then, of course, equal rewards, those items one wished for. This phenomenon would recur each year, and so reinforce the society's practice of the same process year after year: the stimulating of a young mind's belief system by getting a list of wanted things to Santa Claus or to Santa's helpers, being extra careful to seem good especially after submitting said list, and then impatiently waiting until Christmas to discover the arrival of the wonderful items.

Upon reflection of the effects of Christmas on young minds, we can conclude that throughout these years of impressionable childhood, our upbringing has annually conditioned us to learn well this Santa process and accordingly accept this as normal for our society and our culture. Putting together a Christmas list of wants for Santa Claus becomes the norm. To further create a make-believe foundation of Christmas season beliefs, one need only add other magical elements such as flying reindeer to help deliver the presents, and small elves who assist Santa in his workshop located at the North Pole — naturally, the inviting fantasy merely grows further into the young child's consciousness.

With this early conditioning of this seasonal process of receiving wonderful items like toys year after year from an obviously very good and jolly Santa, we might now consider how a child's mind would make room for the notion of religious prayer, since it could seem rather magical as well. As the subject of prayer is probably described as conversation with a good and righteous Being capable of doing many wonderful things for us, so it could follow that a child's mind might understandably make some parallels, for some startling similarities appear. By the act of transferring the figure of Santa to the figure of God, rather sizable problems are presented not only to the mind of a small child but to all of us in the society as a whole. These problems brought about by persistent and consistent conditioning can and do loom ominously over us individually even years later, as we adjust our adult mindsets to fit our reality as we know it to have become.

Distorted perceptions and understandings of the functions of religious prayer in one's life probably lead any list of difficulties arising from a Santa/God parallel or concept. Very young minds may indeed become conditioned to a Santa figure in their impressionable, formative stages of life. To the extent that one behaves annually in presenting a long list of personal wants to this figure hoping earnestly and expectantly to receive these rewards, a personal religious repercussion might follow. A child's list for Christmas almost always will contain self-interest items — products presented in hyped-up fashion in television commercials, retail catalogues or newspaper advertising circulars. The yearly practice tends to focus on one's own self, and perhaps equating the personal wants to actual personal needs, often mistakenly. Basically, the lesson learned and relearned can seem like this: inform that good and wonderful figure of your wants and many or all of your wants will be satisfied. Fairly simple and straightforward process!

Prayer can be defined as talking with God. A halting question may then arise, "How does one talk with God?" This is certainly a very good question.

If one accepts that God is eternal, everlasting, loving, caring, righteous and holy, then one should also concede that human beings, one's self included, are strikingly different in many ways from God: we have to accept that humans are 1) not eternal on this earth but are temporal beings here for some finite length of time, spanning 80-90 years or so; 2) loving and caring at times but regrettably often failing noticeably in our love and care to others; 3) not always righteous to be sure, though possessing admirable and good intentions usually; and 4) not holy, but hopefully growing spiritually toward an ever holier existence in our relationship with God and with others. So we begin our conversation with God at our starting point of humanity's level rather than God's.

The prayers that an individual makes to God comprise talking with God but incorporate much more simply because the person's whole relationship with others and with God is also inescapably a part of the process — in fact, *all that we are* is involved in our prayers to God. Everything that we dream, fear, our thoughts, our actions, etc. — everything is reflected in a genuine conversation with the Eternal, Holy Being to such a point that the focus of the prayer *grows toward God*, and *away from oneself*. One's religious attention therefore grows to God; "*my* will be done" becomes instead "*thy* will be done." In petitioning God's help with some personal problem faced on a daily basis, for example, one most likely may not start a prayer in the mindset of God's will, but in one's own will by earnestly pleading for a remedy for that particular difficulty.

We could say that if a person, in full and complete reverence for God, enters into prayer with a personal agenda, in time the loving, spiritual therapy of God may draw one's will so close to God's will that one's complete submission to God would then bring the two wills together, becoming one . . . God's, that is. This true relating to God offers us all such wonderfully beneficial spiritual resources to deal with our earthly problems that we would naturally desire more and more time with God. However, we should hasten to add that not all problems find neat answers; in other words, some answers do not come right away and of course some do not seem to ever come — yet, we may discover something rather surprising. The closer relationship to God due to prayer may in fact turn out to be the *ends* of the prayers rather than the *means* of prayers. We can come to know that the enhanced relating with the awesome, loving Eternal God supplies us with immense inner peace and hope for better days ahead. While it is true that some of our problems will remain intact as ever, our specific personal perspectives regarding those problems may change in such a way that the problems will not affect us in the same negative ways as before (it has been said before that it is not so important what problems we meet as how we meet them; and that it is not so important what happens *to* us as what happens *within* us). Peace inside one's soul and a genuine hope for better times ahead will prove to be the results of true relating to God. This we all hope for, yearn for, strive for and so need to find time every day. These are the wonderful benefits of real prayer. Childish Christmas list-type prayers that adults often bring to God tend to be selfish. Prayers are not really about the self-interests or the self-centered items we want or things we want done, but are, simply put, about God.

In reaching that place in life of knowing oneness with God in prayer, several things may change. Being at one with God in this spiritual way of love and peace toward God and others around us sometimes quickly thrusts us to a realization that painful issues, past or present, will suddenly come up, like it or not. As painful matters usually point to one's own shortcomings, mistakes or hurtful actions of word or deed, that oneness with God may urge honest reexamination of memories long buried away, hidden from all. Yet, God knows. God knew then, and God knows the point when a person can revisit those areas — areas one would just as soon forget.

Nothing can ultimately be held back from God. If one is in a prayer closely attuned to God spiritually, then that relationship with God draws out from the buried state matters which need to be addressed, confessed, rectified and remedied before God and possibly also before others involved in that pain. A true loving relationship with the Holy Eternal Being will enable one in solemn, reverent, genuine prayerful attention to God to better deal with these really painful matters at some point in life, either now or later. These sudden moments of discovery may indeed feel terrifying and threatening, but to our Eternal God one opens up all of one's soul — wide open for that thorough spiritual healing to take place right there in the soul, where others were not allowed access. The loving, caring Creator God who made us all will confront these matters justly, it is true, but also mercifully and tenderly. After all, God is love. By genuine, honest confession before God, ample forgiveness is graciously, wonderfully and generously given — and yes, felt at the very soul of the praying follower. The Creator God, the God of Peace and Love, bestows with that forgiveness the tremendous inner sense of real oneness with God so that the forgiven person contains ample peace and love to follow God's example and bestow to others peace, love and forgiveness. Genuine relating to God genuinely affects one's relating to others.

There are several different types of prayers. There are prayers of petition, confession, intercession (praying on behalf of someone else than self), praise and thanksgiving. A prayer of petition is that whereby one brings heart-felt needs to the attention of God, and includes a working-through of difficult issues, such as one coming into prayer with self-centered matters involving wants as opposed to personal needs, or a list of complaints keenly and honestly felt. A prayer of confession includes ultimate submission to the will of God in that the follower enters into a true realization of that part of the past or present that misses the mark or falls short of what God would have wished, gratefully receiving divine forgiveness, resolving to turn away from that shortcoming. A prayer of intercession exhibits love and concern for others in its active expression of real needs of others, persons we know or even those we do not know at all. A prayer of praise offers deep spiritual acknowledgment of the goodness, holiness and righteousness of God's love and grace, stating this in worship before God. A prayer of thanksgiving is similar in form to praise as it expresses with gratefulness the bounty of God's grace and love upon oneself and others, an undeserved bounty of riches upon our lives. We could conclude that the full array of this spectrum of prayers will enable us to pursue further spiritual growth in our relationship with Eternal God. Certainly, we can move apart from the prayers of selfishness, a self-centered pleading focusing on "me, me, me," and instead place the focus of our relationship with God upon God. We have yearned for so long a time to be at one with God.

CHAPTER 17

DIFFICULT TIMES

Dear God,

Please accept this prayer of mine. Please accept this prayer even though I am sure I am not knowledgeable or good enough to pray very properly to you. As you are all-powerful, all-knowing, loving and caring, the Eternal Creator God, I pray that my prayer is somehow, some way worthy enough for your hearing. Yet, there are things in this world that trouble me. I do wonder, why bad, sometimes terrible or even horrible, things happen to well-meaning, good people. These things bother me a lot. I cannot find a way to understand why these things happen. And then I wonder, "Am I wrong to wonder about such matters?" Since in your creating us, you gave us all minds to think with as well as hearts to feel with, I do find myself questioning in my mind how a loving, caring God could just allow or permit such horrible human acts of war, killing, torture, spouse abuse or child abuse — or natural acts of deadly hurricanes, earthquakes, tornadoes or floods — or deadly accidental acts like automobile collisions, airplane crashes, drownings or fire . . . these things seem so endless, and so often. The question does not just go away. Why dear God, why do these things happen? These destructive acts really seem to happen most all the time — they have in the past and now in the present. I do not understand.

But, I want to be faithful; my heart yearns to be faithful and my mind yearns to be faithful, too. So, I pray to you. What can I do but pray to God? May my faith be strengthened, somehow, dear God. I pray that in the long run, Eternal God will surely prevail over all these things . . . over everything, over all evil acts in this world. I know my faith needs this assurance; this I realize. So, I pray that over the long haul, over the long run, Eternal God will indeed triumph and prevail over all death and sorrow. Please accept this prayer of mine, dear God. Amen.

While making a visit to the city of Beirut, Lebanon, in May 1997, Pope John Paul II gave a speech which included the following words to large throngs of people. Most were old enough to keenly remember violent times in their city and in their land. "Everyone is invited to engage in the service of peace and reconciliation . . . so violence will never triumph over dialogue, nor fear and caution over confidence, nor hatred over fraternal love."[27]

We all, sadly and regrettably, know of many events, big and small, of violence, fear and hatred in our lifetime. Numerous instances of such events have occasioned our life experiences or of those around us, or of those we may know only indirectly or at a distance by way of some loose connections of circumstances. Yes, time has been marred by violence, fear and hatred. In fact, it has been marred throughout all of time, history tells us. The city of Beirut, known for a long period as a bustling commercial hub of the Middle East, gradually became caught in the war-torn consequences of battling forces of armies and suffered all manner of bombing and destruction. Refugee scenes became commonplace there. Those consequences seemed to last for years and years — it seemed that the violence, fear and hatred just would not go away. Even the name of the city grew to be a synonymous term for an unending, impossible-to-mend, impasse of human violence — a complete breakdown of law and order, and of institutions of any kind.

Over the centuries and centuries of time, the human race has come to know also of the genuine and fervent hope, eternal hope actually, of the concrete belief that *ultimately* "violence will never triumph over dialogue, nor fear and caution over confidence, nor hatred over fraternal love." It is *ultimately* that we are able to hold onto such a conviction that peace and reconciliation will indeed be the victors, since we sadly know all too well of the instances of defeat — those bitter setbacks that affect us. Devastating tragedies, despair and simple hopelessness can always point to an empty future. However, over the long, vast span of time itself God, the eternal Being, is quite aware of our days of defeat and our individual spans of life,

---

[27] John Lancaster, "Beirut's Muslims and Christians Greet Pope, Who Calls for Reconciliation," *The Washington Post* 11 May 1997: A24.

and so greatly loves each one of us, loving thoroughly with complete mercy and forgiveness. With God's love upon us through any such period of defeat and sense of an empty future, we may even begin to discover something rather difficult to quickly accept as true — that is, a genuine confidence. Only the Eternal God can bolster our shaky individual human condition in the most troublesome of times. That genuine inner confidence can be ours if only we recognize it as available, and claim it: firmly holding it dear to the human heart. Confidence in the long run, confidence in the long term, is ours — ours for the taking. Admittedly, setbacks can occur also, but ultimately do not tarnish throughout the long term of life. Knowing this long-term involvement of Eternal God will bolster us during our short term: those moments of great difficulty, whether minutes, hours or even years. Confidence and faith in God will survive and endure through it all, even all the way through the centuries of time itself, not just through our own individual lifespans of human journey. God is God-of-the-long-term, and always will be.

During our individual lifetimes, we fully participate in life as we know it, with all the possible negatives that come along with the all the possible positives. All possibilities appear to be there: our lives can seem subject to the workings of a variety of potential sadness as well as to a variety of potential joys. Yet, through the mix which occurs, the long-term picture that we tend to summarize as we go, peace will win. Now, this may, of course, take a tremendously long period of time to fully convince us all, especially those caught up in the worst of luck, in really dire, unfortunate circumstances offering great sadness and sorrow, or even tragedy of loss — but, this truth of divine peace winning out will indeed prove itself to be the case. Even as some of us will see only empty futures due to losses awfully painful to endure, the Everlasting God will see to it that God will prevail over every negative of human experiences. This is the hope we hold onto which strengthens our faith when nothing else seems to help. God knows. God loves. God will prevail, in the long run.

In our present time the invitation is made: "everyone is invited to engage in the service of peace and reconciliation," even if only with those persons closest to our daily lives, those around us. With those people with whom we have personal contact, we can truly engage in peace-making through our conversations, or merely by listening to others' concerns, or with gentle smiles and acts of kindness. Peace and reconciliation can begin this way. The real peace inside our individual souls can be strengthened with that peace we extend to others around us, in our own piece of the world. We can begin to prove it to ourselves, if only we try. We can believe that God gives us a lifetime in which to test this ourselves.

CHAPTER 18

TO KNOW GOD

To return again to questions already asked and answered is probably a commonplace occurrence for humankind. Maybe this is some measure of our being human. As regards matters concerning Eternal God, God's being and our relating to God, perhaps we never really find ourselves confidently settled with nicely developed answers that completely satisfy all our concerns. Striving to really know God is difficult. Many even profess that an infinite, eternal deity is essentially unknowable, or at the minimum extremely hard to fathom, at least now while we are still in earthly existence, knowing only this world in our life experiences to date.

Some questions persist and insist on lingering with us. "Just who really knows all about God, anyway?" we ask. Do writers of religious books and materials know everything about God? Does the writer of this book know everything about God? Many questions come to mind that bother us. The use of healthy skepticism, regarding religious knowledge, can be beneficial in several ways. We are certainly aware that there have been countless persons throughout history who have made daring claims, such as actually having seen God, actually having heard from God, actually having talked with God, somehow given authority to speak for God, or simply declaring to really know all about God. Claims have been made. Well, who really knows?

We know that many voices today make such claims, even in our own communities. From those who boldly declare to know all the answers to all questions, we simply have to politely remove ourselves, resisting capture so that we can consider such puzzling questions or issues on our own, in our own setting and at our own timing and pace. Allowing ourselves to be captured by loud and persistent voices is to surrender our God-given freedoms to choose and to make decisions for ourselves. We can do worse than relying upon the divine, gentle guidance we can find within our hearts, together with logic from our minds. The loving, caring God permits us a true freedom of religious choices, whereby our individual use of a healthy skepticism may indeed serve us well. We can exercise our freedom to decide for ourselves, where and when and how we may wish. The author of this small book, with a title of *About God*, only intends to offer some questions, some observations, some comments, some fears, some doubts and some attempts at a few possible answers to consider, setting aside many other areas of religious interests. The scope of this book's material is therefore rather limited in that way, but the limited material hopefully can indeed be considered to be about God. Hopefully readers will use God-given skepticism as they wonder about issues and then reflect upon their own relationships with God and with others.

Given the human tendency to be suspicious and skeptical it is easy oftentimes to find ourselves positioned too far, in a rather extreme fashion actually, regarding some aspect of some issue. Regarding the view of God's accessibility to a human being, it may be easy to consider God as much too far off, in some faraway, lofty level — simply too high for any human reach whatsoever. We might feel that the distance between us and God is so great as to be cut off, in a sense, from God's regard for and availability to us. An ancient psalmist's voice expressed something of this notion of God's inaccessibility (from Psalm 144:3-4). "O LORD, what are human beings that you regard them, or mortals that you think of them? They are like breath; their days are like a passing shadow."

Such an ancient voice may offer an idea which can sound familiar to many today, since it is common to feel small, unimportant, or simply irrelevant in our giant, fast-paced and rapidly-changing environment. Why should God even bother with a mere individual or even give one a passing thought? In fact, mortals can be viewed with the idea of inconsequence, as a puff of air and our lifespan compared to fleeting of a passing shadow. How small, unimportant and irrelevant this imagery sounds. Yet, we must realize, in fact we have to continue to keep ourselves in the mindset, that the Creator God created us all out of love, wanting and hoping for love in return. This loving, creative act implies an actual relationship, as we are made in the Creator's image. We and God are related! To recall this is to remind ourselves that we are not small, unimportant or irrelevant in God's eyes. Human spirits can rejoice that we certainly are much, much more than breath and that our days are much more in importance to our God than a mere passing shadow. The loving, caring Creator God offers us all that personal relationship with which we can expect God's attention and not a simple, cold and distant indifference. For God to be disdainful and to take no interest in our well-being is to be at complete odds with our understanding of a creator God/created human relationship. The idea of a disinterested, unconcerned God is conceptually incompatible with our understanding, and it certainly should be rejected out of hand as unhelpful and inappropriate — its inaccuracy ought to be held as absolute. God cares. God loves.

However, problems occur out of our understanding of relating with a personal God. A loving, caring God does not always appear to be helpful or available to meet our needs when we expect and may feel the needs so intensely. Too often we feel that God is not revealing any help whatsoever to our obvious and genuine needs. "Why doesn't God respond to fervent prayers?" we can ask rather often — too often, it seems. We cannot be faulted for assuming that a loving God should answer honest, intense requests to meet our most urgent needs. We can turn to the psalmist who dared to utter concerns like these so long ago, expressing the same questions . . . centuries-old questions (from Psalm 80:3-7).

> Restore us, O God; let your face shine that we may be saved.
> O LORD God of hosts, How long will you be angry with your people's prayers? You have fed them with the bread of tears, and given them tears to drink in full measure. You make us the scorn of our neighbors; our enemies laugh among themselves.
> Restore us, O God of hosts; let your face shine,
> that we may be saved.

This old passage calls out with such imagery as letting God's face to shine upon us, whereby the mere direction of God's attention to God's people will, in and of itself, save them in their particular troubles. The actual attention from God is expectant help to our human needs, the thinking goes. Human beings have expected this from God many centuries ago and we expect the same today — restore us, help us, provide answers or information which we truly and oftentimes desperately need in our lives. Surely we require to know how to function well with our relationships here on earth since complicated, tangled problems, maybe quite serious ones regrettably, will ensnare us away from normal day-to-day routines. Unfortunately, pain, suffering and death touch our lives and those lives close to us, whether relatives, neighbors, friends or co-workers. Certain difficult times require more from us spiritually to continue on and to manage well through such experiences. They are the times when we find ourselves turning to God for help. We ourselves may not feel adequate to deal with life as it presents itself sometimes; we may feel we have only limited resources or limited vision to handle some acute pressing situation. Perhaps, we will probably discover some real resources available nearby — yet, even these may prove to be incomplete, as very troubling situations demand so much and can drain so much out of us. To turn then to God for real help is natural and necessary for our well-being: we can pray as others have done long before us, "restore us, O God, let your face shine."

Today, we realize that instances of pain, suffering and death are unavoidable and integral parts of life. Times such as these greatly try our souls and test our faith, as we wonder about great matters not only regarding life itself, but also about relationships with others and with God. As we ponder large, subjective kinds of questions, no one around may provide satisfying or complete answers. Really satisfying responses may only be found within one's own heart; however, complete answers might even then prove to be elusive and unavailable altogether. Life's disappointments and sorrows do not always present nice, neat and complete solutions as questions can linger indefinitely. It is natural to feel unable to get a handle on things when we have little control over situations close at hand. We simply do not have all answers. In the first century the apostle Paul wrote to a group of early followers (from 1 Corinthians 13:12): "For now we see in a mirror, dimly, but then we will see face to face. Now I know only in part; then I will know fully, even as I have been fully known." It would appear that there are limitations between us and our knowledge of God. There are limitations to what others who are available to advise or counsel us have in their understanding of God's ways and in their knowledge of divine matters. This human knowledge of God is, at best, incomplete; this is not to say that human knowledge about God is woefully inadequate but that it is quite limited when compared to that which we will understand in our future life with God. Now in a mirror, so to speak, we may see dimly, in that we presently know about God with knowledge that is indirect and partial. Upon meeting our Creator God after this life, we shall know fully, understanding all knowledge about God directly and completely. No dim light, but actually seeing face-to-face! We can assume we will receive truly satisfying answers to the most troubling questions, absolutely complete answers to the most elusive of matters. More importantly, though, we shall in our face-to-face knowing, know God — just as we are presently fully known by our God.

To answer that initial question, "Who really knows all about God?" possibly our best answer is that no one presently on earth knows. With the words of the apostle Paul still sounding in our ears, we can settle on the belief that upon seeing God we shall know, just not now. Probably this partly explains our insatiable yearning for God and our calling upon the name of God to come into our specific time and space. This intense urging and longing is not something new; centuries-old voices expressed the same utterances. The psalmists of the Old Testament offered these words long ago, expressing an urgent longing, a passionate desire for God (from Psalm 63:1-4).

> O God, you are my God, I seek you,
> my soul thirsts for you; my flesh faints for you,
> as in a dry and weary land where there is no water.
> So I have looked upon you in the sanctuary, beholding
> your power and glory.
> Because your steadfast love is better than life,
> my lips will praise you.
> So I will bless you as long as I live;
> I will lift up my hands and call on your name.

This psalmist voiced the longing for God in the heartfelt context of love, of being loved by God. As God's love is described here as "steadfast," it is judged to be even better than life itself. As love in our own lifetimes can oftentimes appear conditional and temporal, God's divine love is obviously quite different — steadfast, even to the point of being much better than any love known in this life here on earth. Then perhaps it is no real wonder that the human longing for a God with this love can be so intense and powerful that one enters into a worshipful manner before God. What other response can one offer but that of true worship? God's divine love, by its very nature, stirs this kind of response from the longing human spirit (from Psalm 31:3-5). "You are indeed my rock and my fortress; for your name's sake lead me and guide me, take me out of the net that is hidden for me, for you are my refuge. Into your hand I commit my spirit; you have redeemed me, O LORD, faithful God."

A follower of God can understandably long to cling to God as if to a rock, and to rush to God as if toward a fortress to guard against the dire difficulties of our earthly lives. God is easily thought of as a refuge, for we surely and eagerly take refuge when beset with anguishing troubles. Such imagery offers a picture of outlasting a nasty, violent storm until the unsettled weather is past. The notion of safe protective shelter awaiting us convincingly invites the human spirit toward God without any long decision-making process. "Into your hand I commit my spirit . . . you have redeemed me." It is this communication of God's goodness and genuine offer of divine love which we instinctively and thoroughly trust.

By experiencing our God we naturally wish to know this God even more than we do, wanting to know all about God, even everything about God. It is in experiencing God through our relationship in life that we come to know God (from Psalm 23).

> The LORD is my shepherd, I shall not want.
> He makes me lie down in green pastures;
> he leads me beside still waters; he restores my soul.
> He leads me in right paths for his name's sake.
> Even though I walk through the darkest valley, I fear no evil; for you are with me;
> your rod and your staff — they comfort me.
> You prepare a table before me
> in the presence of my enemies;
> you anoint my head with oil;
> my cup overflows.
> Surely goodness and mercy shall follow me
> all the days of my life,
> and I shall dwell in the house of the LORD
> my whole life long.

CHAPTER 19

MADE TO BE HUMAN

Numerous religious authors have long written of the "human predicament" and our human journey under God's care. Human beings have pondered from our earliest beginnings just where we fit into the big scheme of things. Merely by observing about our surroundings in this world, we can drift off into reflection upon questions that confront our life journey here on this planet. One contemporary writer expresses our human questions in a most interesting and direct way.

> What does it mean to be a human being? What is our position in this universe? These age-old questions are asked with renewed strength and intensity today. . . . Reading the daily newspapers and watching the news on TV we indeed gain the impression that there is something fundamentally out of balance with the world we live in. We seem to have lost our sense of orientation and direction on our cosmic journey. The firm foundation on which to build our lives has disappeared from our sight. Our world is in turmoil and our lives are threatened by the impact of technology that made our lives more changeable than ever and increased the pace in modern living to such an extent that truly "our years come to an end like a sigh" (Psalm 90:9). We have domesticated the world in an unprecedented way, but we have lost our souls and each other in the process. At no point in history have we had so much knowledge about the world that surrounds us and so little insight into our own place in this world and so little understanding for each other.[28]

---

[28] Hans Schwarz, *Our Cosmic Journey* (Minneapolis: Augsburg, 1977) 13.

As we find ourselves today facing such an old question as "What does it mean to be a human being?" we might strive to develop a further insight and understanding by approaching the Christian view of humans as "made in the image of God." We might wonder, quite literally actually, what on earth does that mean? What a daunting notion for us to fathom, viewing ourselves as in the image of God, while we live and breathe in the midst of our sinful human histories, both individually and also collectively as groups and nations. We may surely consider that we are quite a sinful lot — and the level of the image of God seems rather lofty, high above our heads. To approach this idea we might benefit by first considering some roles and functions which we believe God exhibits in relating to us and to the world as a whole.

Our Eternal God might be said to possess many roles and perform many functions in dealing with human beings throughout our history. In a most basic way we may understand God as Creator, Redeemer and Sustainer. Before God became the Redeemer (redeeming our fallen, sinful selves) and Sustainer (encouraging us and lifting our spirits up to know the hope and comfort of divine peace) God was first the Creator. God created us all, male and female, so it was written long ago, breathing life into us. The Creator God formed us and thus knows us intimately well, understands us and maybe even believes in us. Yes, we can affirm that God is surely involved creatively in us.

> Since God is experienced and understood as creatively involved with human and world history as its initiator, granter, and redeemer, he can endow human destiny with eternal significance. In the light of God, humanity is not just a link in the natural context, but with its peculiarly human features it gains significance as God's administrator in this world.
>
> ... The experience of a God who cares endows our existence with meaning, and, at the same time, permits us to understand the whole world as God's creation. The world was not created for our exploitation or self-glorification. Our uniquely human position notwithstanding, the cosmos was created together with us to enjoy God and to be enjoyed by him forever.[29]

To continue our attempts to understand ourselves in the Christian idea as made in the image of God, we may also note some aspects of the Christian view towards the being of God. From the earliest Christian era, a view

---

[29] Schwarz 267-268, 269.

developed and became in time accepted, by and large by most of the faithful (though not without controversy). That idea was of the "trinity," or one triune being, or God as three-in-one. This trinity was namely God the Father, Jesus Christ the Son and the Holy Spirit. This was not a developed concept at first, as it was quite vague until about the 4th century. As the divine being of an infinite, eternal God may appear overwhelming to the finite human mind, the notion of thinking of God in different dimensions was helpful: Father or Abba (meaning "daddy" actually), Son referring to Jesus as Christ, and Holy Spirit or Spirit of God. This basic view of God has been held ever since — that the Eternal God exists in three persons, yet still one God, or one substance. Theologians have long discussed the trinity idea and devoted much time and energy in considering how we may appropriately think of the being of God. Noted theologians still debate aspects of the trinity and its "formula."

> Thus God makes himself known as one-in-three, three-in-one. He must be conceived as simultaneously Father (God-as-transcendent), Son (having a particular definite character and being, as seen in historical person-event Jesus Christ), and the Holy Spirit (present in and to and with us in our world). The absence of any of these dimensions to God's being (as we necessarily conceive that being) would mean that we are not conceiving of the God who reveals himself in Jesus Christ.[30]

> The formula of one substance and three persons constitute an interpretation that has ceased to communicate, for it talks the language and moves in the discourse of an absolute philosophy. This does not mean, however, that the formula has to be rejected . . . what is required is a new act of interpretation that will interpret in a contemporary language this ancient and hallowed formula of the Church.[31]

We can now consider the task of attempting some new way or formula, "a new act of interpretation . . . in a contemporary language." Given our natural innermost yearning to know God more fully, we can wonder in total awe of God's being, and, in absolute and utter reverence for God, search our vocabulary with hopes to reflect more closely the dimensions of our Eternal God, an infinite being, for our finite minds. We accept the one-in-three and

---

[30] Gordon Kaufman, *Systematic Theology* (New York: Scribner, 1969) 99.
[31] John Macquarrie, *Principles of Christian Theology*, 2nd ed. (New York: Scribner, 1977) 192.

three-in-one concept to be helpful, but perhaps only up to some point: we can allow ourselves to use that concept as a basis or beginning point in reflecting upon God anew. Reassured through God's loving approval, we can offer our human attempts to each other and up to God, hoping they may prove helpful in some manner to strengthen understanding of our faith. We should welcome all attempts to know God more fully, in our verbal language which we have to use.

Dimensions

Depth, Height and Width . . .
dimensions . . . Divine essence, all.
yet, unbounded measure, immense and vast.
a triune Being, by name of God.

the very Depth within a soul.
deepest place within each one.
only the Creator fully knows,
that part created, innermost, all.
the Depth within: Abba.
an innermost depth . . . a dimension.

the very Height among flesh.
upon the face of the earth.
only the Incarnate, Immanuel,
the God-with-us, among us all.
the Height of human fullness: Christ.
a height at a cross . . . a dimension.

the very Width spread throughout.
the Comforter, Counselor, now far and wide.
only the Holy Spirit could so move,
as breath, or wind, reaching us all.
the Width moving around us: Spirit.
a width in movement . . . a dimension.

> Depth, Height and Width . . .
> dimensions . . . Divine essence, all.
> yet, unbounded measure, immense and vast.
> a triune Being, by name of God.

Given our finite human attempts to express verbally our view of the very being of our eternal, infinite God, we in like manner may now consider ourselves — and in the image of that God. Believing God to be viewing our efforts from above, we struggle in our finite human attempts to find "a new act of interpreting in a contemporary language" to more closely reflect ourselves. To that daunting idea of being made in the image of God, a God of different dimensions, we might return to the same notion of three-in-one and apply it to ourselves: as we have historically viewed God as three persons in one substance, maybe we can also view ourselves in like manner — since we are in God's image.

Obviously the notions of body, mind and spirit can indeed be plausible dimensions of our being; these aspects of three dimensions have been well developed in our history. Upon further reflection, possibilities could include a slightly varied formulation: we may offer one which seems to amplify our relationship with God (and as was the earlier example, this too is merely one human attempt which we can offer to ourselves and to God). We can name these three: our better selves, our worse selves and our indifferent selves. As these dimensions of our being surely relate to God by our human yearning for, crying to, responding to and loving God in addition to simply disobeying God or just ignoring God altogether in our lives, it is our *relationship* with the living God which is directly focused upon. This realization hits home because in the final analysis we simply cannot hide our selves from the eternal God who is looking down, seeing our relationship with God and how that relationship shapes our lives.

Dimensions of Our Selves

better, worse and indifferent . . .
our selves . . . human essence, all.
yet, complicated being, resting and restless.
a being of God, by name of human.

our better selves, the good from within.
creative, loving and hopeful with all.
we know God; and knowing godliness.
God uplifts us, Spirit encourages us.
we respond to God, God responds to us:
        God loves us, weeps in joy.

our worse selves, the missing the mark.
greedy, self-seeking and denying to all.
we knew God; and knowing sinfulness.
God calls for us, Spirit reminds us.
we respond to God, God responds to us:
        God loves us, weeps in understanding.

our indifferent selves, the complete withdrawal.
hollow, abandoning and void of all.
we ignore God; and knowing hopelessness.
God tries to reach us, Spirit tries to remind.
we won't respond to God, God responds to us:
        God loves us, weeps in anguish.

better, worse and indifferent . . .
our selves . . . human essence, all.
yet, complicated being, resting and restless.
a being of God, by name of human.

We are called to reflect and wonder. As human beings, we will most naturally think about our relationship with God. From any consideration of the being of God and also of ourselves, what might we conclude regarding the idea of being made in the image of God? First of all, more exhaustive reflection would certainly be called for, bringing in many other disciplines to bear. Also, much more time to absorb, process and consider would surely benefit us. We need to wonder. Ultimately, though, the very best answer might be that we simply are not yet at that level of sufficient and adequate understanding. We still strive for that level: we are on our journey, seeking God.

    We continue on that journey.

    We continue walking.

CHAPTER 20

JESUS OF NAZARETH AT ONE WITH GOD

One prominent figure of Christianity who absolutely requires specific consideration in human thinking of the divine God is the one included in the three personhood of God. The oneness of God cannot be adequately considered without dealing with some aspects of the person of Jesus of Nazareth. For centuries, the efforts of relating the personhood of Jesus to the oneness of God has been a truly exhaustive and lengthy theological endeavor for diverse thinkers, knowledgeable theologians and biblical scholars alike. Any consideration here is mere "tip of the iceberg" discussion; yet, some areas, of course, demand at least some attention. The person of Jesus has had a most profound impact upon the world, such that even the oneness of God includes this individual Jesus.

The person of Jesus was, of course, born a Jew in early first century Palestine of the Middle East. Tradition has held that he was a carpenter from a small town of Nazareth in the Galilee region. He became a traveling teacher and preacher of his ministry, covering surrounding villages and towns. In so doing he acquired a popular reputation and his comments were quite outspoken. However, his activities soon earned him much hostility from the established Jewish religious leaders. He was deemed a dangerous challenger to the religious status quo. The religious authorities began developing ways to discredit Jesus, and later on to put an end to him and his work altogether. By insisting on the ruling Roman authorities to try him for crimes, they had him turned over to the Roman rulers for eventual death by the cruel and painful way of crucifixion, as the Roman occupation used at that time. Surely, both the Jewish and Roman leaders believed their problem of this person Jesus was then over, and with his death his influence would obviously be behind them once and for all.³²

In a consideration of Jesus, one encounters great difficulty in separating the work and the person. The very person of Jesus, his identity, has been an integral part of his work, as biblical accounts provide much of his own claims as to who in fact he actually was: yes, he was an actual human being with many normal, common experiences characteristic of us all; however, he obviously claimed much more. His identity, according to biblical accounts as affirmed by Jesus himself in his teachings, included: the Son of God, the Messiah (or Christ), the fulfillment of Old Testament promises, the Son of man, Savior, Lord, and also one with authority to forgive sins.³³

With news of Jesus' actual physical death on the cross, the biblical accounts record his followers as, initially and quite understandably, despondent and disillusioned. Yet, as they witnessed his startling reappearance to many of them as quite alive and no longer dead, they became powerfully electrified in their energy and beliefs in Jesus as Christ. As this Jesus was certainly not like any other human, his identity shaped the Christian thinking of his early followers and all further development in history of his teaching while he was here on earth.

As the early church grew in its excitement, outwardly to include new followers in other nearby areas and countries, the early understanding of Jesus as Christ began to directly influence development of our human relationship with God. Creator God, through the work and person of Jesus as Christ, expressed the complete depths of divine love for God's created humanity by God's bold act of incarnation, the actual physical embodiment of God's spiritual essence right here on earth in the flesh. Somehow, God in human form was the incarnate Jesus, as Christ. This uniqueness further developed Christian thinking to the point where the trinity idea of God became universally well accepted. The early church's understanding of Jesus as Christ had grown substantially from his ministry days as a Jew in Palestine: not just a mere respected teacher, or even a renowned preacher, or even a highly revered prophet — this Jesus was Christ! Conception of the being of God was dramatically changed in the minds of human beings, due to this one person.

---

[32] Howard Marshall, "Who Was Jesus?" *Eerdman's Handbook to Christian Belief*, ed. Robin Keeley (Grand Rapids: Wm. B. Eerdman's Publishing Co., 1982), 54.
[33] Marshall 62-63.

Noted thinkers soon realized how troubling certain problems were in considering the place afforded a human being in the identity of a divine God, such as how Jesus Christ could be both true man and true God, and yet really just one person. The whole idea of a person acquiring divinity was in all likelihood as confusing as it seemed disturbing. "Was Jesus half human and half divine?" was one question. In the first few centuries, Christian thinkers had to deal with all manner of divine/human issues in order to achieve some acceptable solution for these problems. In the early 4th century, a noted church leader named Arius became a focal point for controversy when he gained some following by teaching that the Father alone was true God, thus denying Jesus Christ's true divinity. This controversy pressured the Church to deal definitively with the issue of Jesus' identity. By the year 451 the Church conclusively decided upon a statement which has remained basic to the Christian faith ever since — that is, that the person of Jesus as Christ was *both fully God and fully human*.[34]

However, this definition has not been completely satisfying. Some discussion continued beyond the year 451 within the Church regarding Jesus having two natures. Today, the idea of being both fully God as well as fully human at the same time may appear to be impossible to comprehend: yet, some might argue, it is precisely because of this difficulty that we can see the uniqueness of the individual Jesus in all of recorded history — for no one other than one with such an identity as Christ could be so difficult to fathom. Actually only God, and not human beings, could thoroughly grasp just how one individual could be fully God and fully human.

Other titles describing Jesus' identity could also be pointed out. He was often said to have been called "Rabbi," or teacher, by Jewish listeners responding to his teachings; or "Immanuel," meaning "God is with us," referring to prophecy which pointed to the birth of Christ; or "Pioneer," an idea offered in the New Testament Letter to the Hebrews, meaning "one who goes before us;" and "Mediator," by modern era theologians referring to an individual as a channel of mediation through which the truth of God has come.

Possibly one of the most significant ideas to present for consideration is that no one title alone for Jesus may be sufficient. All of these mentioned plus

---

[34] Marshall 76.

others can contribute to our understanding of who he in fact was, both for the time period then as well as for us all today. The differing titles add, in their own individual ways, a verbal imagery or picture by which to study the subject in a fresh way. Considering Jesus in several seemingly unrelated terms is to view his person in some manner as to enlighten us further still in God's revelatory ways to reach us. God is not limited to our finite terminology — but through our own human contributions of wording, God can turn them around to reach us in spiritual depths anew. Any new verbal renderings to the person of Jesus, or to the personhood of God for that matter, if offered in reverence, may edify our understanding of just who and how our idea of God's oneness may be expressed. None of these terms may replace the decisive rendering of the Church back in 451 AD of Jesus as both fully God and fully human, but they might supplement the Church's definition with an expanded imagery in hopes to capture more completely or adequately that which is hard to discern by anyone other than God.

A neat, simple way to categorize Jesus of Nazareth into the oneness of our God is obviously complicated and difficult at best. The apostle Paul in writing to early Christians gave the following statements(Philippians 2:5-11):

> Christ Jesus, who, though he was in the form of God, did not regard equality with God as something to be exploited, but emptied himself, taking the form of a slave, being born in human likeness. And being found in human form, he humbled himself and became obedient to the point of death — even death on a cross. Therefore God also highly exalted him and gave him the name that is above every other name, so that at the name of Jesus every knee should bend, in heaven and on earth and under the earth, and every tongue should confess that Jesus Christ is Lord, to the glory of God the Father.

A neat, simple explanation is indeed rather cumbersome. Yes, of course, he was an actual human person who lived here on earth — he breathed, ate and slept like us all, and in these ways was indistinguishable from the rest of us. But his work and identity defined him for all time, distinguishing him from all others as a unique individual in history, unique forevermore. Jesus has become, through the intervening love of Creator God, our Lord, Savior and Christ. For countless numbers, Jesus as Christ has entered their hearts in other ways such as teacher, Rabbi, Immanuel, Pioneer, or as Mediator. In this context, we all may find him in our different, individual ways. We may know him best simply in the terms and ways he has affected us most keenly, mysteriously riveting us to his person. Complicated; yes. He is . . . as we know him. Simple as that.

Chapter 21

Spirit of God

A paradox exists for our attempts at reflecting upon God.

On the one hand, we conceive of God as many things — as an infinite, personal, eternal, uncreated, loving, caring reality, who as Creator God has brought about everything that is, and who as Sustainer God has revealed to created humanity a wondrously divine love and presence. On the other hand, because of the vast and overwhelming nature of the amazing divine reality, we can only stand back in silent awe . . . or more probably, we bow, or fall, before God's commanding, holy presence. We are awestruck. Our concept of God is great. God seems indescribable since we cannot really find words which are adequate and sufficient enough to express our belief of God's being in an accurate way (from Isaiah 40:18-23, 25-26).

> To whom then will you liken God,
> or what likeness compare with him?
> An idol? — A workman casts it,
> and a goldsmith overlays it with gold,
> and casts for it silver chains.
> As a gift one chooses mulberry wood
> — wood that will not rot —
> then seeks out a skilled artisan
> to set up an image that will not topple.
>
> Have you not known? Have you not heard?
> Has it not been told you from the beginning?

> Have you not understood from the foundations of the earth?
> It is he who sits above the circle of the earth,
> and its inhabitants are like grasshoppers;
> who stretches out the heavens like a curtain,
> and spreads them like a tent to live in;
> who brings princes to naught,
> and makes the rulers of the earth as nothing.
>
> To whom then will you compare me,
> or who is my equal? says the Holy One.
> Lift up your eyes on high and see:
> Who created these?
> He who brings out their host and numbers them,
> calling them all by name;
> because he is great in strength,
> mighty in power, not one is missing.

It is in this context of understanding God as being so lofty and so high above us all in divine holiness and righteousness that we may make an amazing discovery. Yes, we are aware that Holy God is indeed totally overwhelming in eternity and infinite love — but this same God comes to us individually! God enters into our time and space as a spiritual reality within our hearts and minds in a way so as to not overwhelm us with God's terrifyingly great power — oftentimes entering as a small voice within. Such a tiny voice is available if only we cease our loud clamor of excited outbursts and instead move apart to experience the stillness of God's reaching out to us in the solitude and privacy of our inner realm. This inner realm is the area where God's spirit enters and dwells within us. No longer solely existing in the high and lofty domain with overwhelming holiness above us, but God's spirit is now with us on our level, right here on earth, right within our hearts and minds. We can conceptualize that the spirit of God is now alongside the beating human heart and the seeking, yearning mind. It seems we often clamor to seek God in many distant places but fail to comprehend that God is easily found — that God actually dwells within us already. God is so close to us, and has been all along. The ancient psalmist gives us this passage, from Psalm 139:1-18:

O LORD, you have searched me and known me.
You know when I sit down and when I rise up;
you discern my thoughts from far away.
You search out my path and my lying down,
and are acquainted with all my ways.
Even before a word is on my tongue,
O LORD, you know it completely.
You hem me in, behind and before,
and lay your hand upon me.
Such knowledge is too wonderful for me;
it is so high that I cannot attain it.

Where can I go from your spirit?
Or where can I flee from your presence?
If I ascend to heaven, you are there;
if I make my bed in Sheol, you are there.
If I take the wings of the morning
and settle at the farthest limits of the sea,
even there your hand shall lead me,
and your right hand shall hold me fast.
If I say, "Surely the darkness shall cover me,
and the light around me become night"
even the darkness is not dark to you;
the night is as bright as the day,
for darkness is as light to you.

For it was you who formed my inward parts;
you knit me together in my mother's womb.
I praise you, for I am fearfully and wonderfully made.
Wonderful are your works; that I know very well.
My frame was not hidden from you,
when I was being made in secret,
intricately woven in the depths of the earth.
Your eyes beheld my unformed substance.
In your book were written
all the days that were formed for me,

> when none of them as yet existed.
> How weighty to me are your thoughts, O God!
> How vast is the sum of them!
> I try to count them — they are more than the sand;
> I come to the end — I am still with you.

Coming originally from the Latin verb "to breathe," the word "spirit" means breath or wind. In a physical sense, we know that without breath there can be no life, since it is obviously essential and a natural sign of life. Our health depends on the conditions created by continual breathing. So it is the case with the believer, in the religious sense. Without the presence of the Divine Spirit within, the believer is lifeless — or in other words, dispirited. With the Spirit of God within the individual, the relationship of the created human being with the Creator God instantly manifests itself, allowing immediacy of this dimension to our lives. We can affirm the Holy Spirit provides us our personal reflecting necessary to draw God into our time and space. God is definitely present with the believer, not merely thought of as far away in the lofty, high, other-worldly place far removed from mere human beings. God, who is spirit, is as close to us as our breath.

In a practical manner, however, human beings in our modern days of fast-paced activities routinely encounter many obstacles and difficulties which hinder truly reflective living involving God's spirit in our inner being. The daily outside world rarely offers an uncluttered occasion for inner retreat, but rather the hectic commonplace circumstances of numerous responsibilities and obligations pulling at us. Such is a more typical work environment for the majority of our "age of anxiety." Claire M. Brissette, in her book *Reflective Living: A Spiritual Approach to Everyday Life*, provides us this setting which can characterize our lives as always caught up in the rush of activities and demands in everyday life:

> We have responsibilities to fulfill; decisions to make; projects to carry out; meals to prepare; appointments to keep. In the midst of everyday busyness, it is relatively easy to become preoccupied and fragmented. We may come to see our various responsibilities as so many isolated compartments of our lives, just so many obligations to fulfill before we can take time to live. As we run busily from one task to another, we risk losing ourselves and consequently bringing to daily responsibilities, as well as to the persons with

whom we live and work, an impoverished self, a self that is continuously pouring itself out, without taking the time to be nourished.[35]

Without adequate time to honestly reflect upon and "process" the variety of experiences thrust upon us in our preoccupied workdays, we miss valuable moments examining and clarifying those experiences and our feelings and responses involved with them. We can rather quickly become burdened with so much disjointed, eventful everyday stuff, and lose sight of the big picture of who we are and God's eternal place in our lives. Without provision for time to reflect with our spiritual selves we may in fact discover we lead an unbalanced life — for the "rat-race" of a hectic, typical day can prove to be an unbalanced atmosphere in which to function.

> It leaves no time for the silence, the withdrawal, the quiet attention to the spiritual, which is essential. . . . They that wait upon the Lord shall renew their strength. In quietness and confidence shall be your strength. These are practical statements; addressed, not to specialists but to ordinary men and women, with a normal psycho-physical make-up. They are literally true now, or can be if we choose. They do not involve any peculiar training, or unnatural effort.[36]

Actually, common sense and logic can probably address the most typical needs for the spiritual side of our lives, even within the workplace. A little silence, in small doses, frequently interspersed in the trying pace of busy routines, can perhaps go a long way to bring cherished benefit — it is also in many cases easy to do, without any drastic measures. Small instances of silence together with faithfulness, kindness and courage surely contribute to the quality of our world of daily activities. This may be almost impossible in some work sectors, but will prove possible, with practice, in many others. Workers fully concentrating upon the constant struggle for material advantage in their employment generally fail to perceive the spiritual reflection that God certainly can be believed to have in mind for us. The apostle Paul wrote of contrasting environments when he urged believers to live by the Spirit (from

---

[35] Claire M. Brissette, *Reflective Living: A Spiritual Approach to Everyday Living* (Whitinsville: Affirmation, 1983) 19.
[36] Evelyn Underhill, *The Life of the Spirit and the Life of Today* (San Francisco: Harper & Row, 1986) 156.

Galatians 5:22,23,25): "The fruit of the Spirit is love, joy, peace, patience, kindness, generosity, faithfulness, gentleness, and self-control. . . . If we live by the Spirit, let us also be guided by the Spirit."

Personal spirituality is as meaningful today as it was back in the first century. The fruits are within the reach of anyone who strives enough to make that daily effort to reflect. We may come to know benefits obtained in our workplace and also away from our place of work. God's spirit-filled relating will effect all manner of relationships in our lives. Christian belief also holds that the work of God's Spirit is not some temporary, momentary circumstance of short-term reality. As God is God-of-the-long-term, we can know the true relating with divine spirit for the whole of our lives.

> To be filled with the Spirit is never a once-for-all experience, on the strength of which we can live for the rest of our lives. . . . We come on times of need and suffering that send us back to God for new resources. . . .
>
> We need to be reassured, not once but over and over again, that we are God's loved and accepted children and heirs. In all these situations we need to open ourselves to a new filling of the same Holy Spirit . . . .[37]
>
> It will certainly bring into life new zest and new meaning; a widening of the horizon and consciousness of security; a fresh sense of joys to be had and of work to be done. The real spiritual consciousness is positive and constructive in type: it does not look back on the past sins and mistakes of the individual or of the community, but in its other-world faith and this-world charity is inspired by a forward-moving spirit of hope.[38]

This available resource for our spiritual well-being can be deemed as absolutely essential to the believer in our modern "age of anxiety." However, we may need reminding that an inner world of quiet spiritual reflection should not replace our everyday life of work; almost all of us are bound for economic reasons to the requirements of our employment.

> Living reflectively is a means of discovering life in and through everyday responsibilities. Life is not what happens after all these obligations have been

---

[37] Tom Smail, "Life in the Holy Spirit," *Eerdman's Handbook to Christian Belief*, ed. Robin Keeley (Grand Rapids: Wm. B. Eerdman's Publishing Co., 1982), 376.
[38] Underhill 170.

fulfilled. Rather, life includes whatever unfolds in and through everyday busyness. Life is at the heart of the stuff of everyday responsibilities. It is there that we continue to touch our limits and strengths, to be called forth and stretched beyond ourselves; there that we touch our human brokenness and frailty, and can allow ourselves to be healed. . . . In the midst of our everyday busyness is hidden the secret of who we are and of who God is calling each of us to become.[39]

The spiritual writer Henri Nouwen has contributed greatly to Christian understanding of what it means to live a spiritual life. In his book *Making All Things New*, Nouwen offers similar emphasis but adds insightful cautions for guidance.

> The spiritual life is not a life before, after, or beyond our everyday existence. No, the spiritual life can only be real when it is lived in the midst of the pains and joys of the here and now.
>
> To be lifted up into the divine life of the Father, the Son, and the Holy Spirit does not mean . . . to be taken out of the world. On the contrary, those who have entered into the spiritual life are precisely the ones who are sent into the world to continue and fulfill the work that Jesus began. The spiritual life does not remove us from the world but leads us deeper into it. . . . It is a life in which we are totally transformed by the Spirit of love. Yet it is a life in which everything seems to remain the same. To live a spiritual life does not mean that we must leave our families, give up our jobs, or change our ways of working; it does not mean that we have to withdraw from social or political activities, or lose interest in literature and art; it does not require severe forms of asceticism or long hours of prayer. Changes such as these may in fact grow out of our spiritual life, and for some people radical decisions may be necessary. But the spiritual life can be lived in as many ways as there are people. . . . What is new is that we are set free from the compulsions of our world and have set our hearts on the only necessary thing. What is new is that we no longer experience the many things, people, and events as endless causes for worry, but begin to experience them as the rich variety of ways in which God makes his presence known to us. . . . Our conflicts and pains, our tasks and promises, our families and friends, our activities and projects, our hopes and aspirations, no longer appear to us as a fatiguing variety of things which we can barely keep together. . . . This does not mean that the spiritual life makes things easier or takes our struggles and pains away. The lives of

---

[39] Brissette 20.

Jesus' disciples clearly show that suffering does not diminish because of conversion. Sometimes it even becomes more intense.

Prayer is first and foremost the active presence of the Holy Spirit in our personal and communal lives. Through the disciplines of solitude and community we try to remove - slowly, gently, yet persistently - the many obstacles which prevent us from listening to God's voice within us. . . . The beginning of the spiritual life is often difficult not only because the powers which cause us to worry are so strong but also because the presence of God's Spirit seems barely noticeable. . . . When we remain attentive to this divine presence, we will be led always deeper into the kingdom. There, to our joyful surprise, we will discover that all things are being made new.[40]

---

[40] Henri J. M. Nouwen, *Making All Things New: An Invitation to the Spiritual Life* (San Francisco: Harper & Row, 1981) 21, 54-58, 90-95.

CHAPTER 22

UNCERTAINTIES AND TRUST

Today it seems that many people in their everyday living report that their faith with God really boils down to something akin to a very simple claim of assurance, let us say, a blessed assurance. This assurance is of such a nature that they appear to cling to it very tightly and point to it often, if not almost always. When pressed regarding some matters of the faith, their replies invariably sound much the same — like a resolute claim to a blessed assurance. In essence, it seems that the repeated response given is the underlying basis of faith — a rather simplified answer to many matters of faith.

To be assured of a blessing or to be lovingly reassured time and time again can certainly strengthen one's faith amid some difficult and trying occasions in life's journey. Yet, the human tendency of clinging, grasping and clutching brief snippets of words or phrases cannot completely sustain us through the utter complexities of life's uneasy and anxious spiritual trials. The world as we know it appears too full of the unpredictable, the mysterious and the unknowable. Such unexpected and unwanted occasions present us with risks that we simply have to contend with intelligently and probably spiritually as well. A simplistic faith characterized primarily as a "blessed assurance" may indeed be a basis for trust in better outcomes, and may of course be quite adequate for young minds; but the maturing minds of adulthood require much more than a quick and simple answer to life's struggles. Life often hurls too many tortuous trials, dilemmas and heavy questions at us for simple answers to shield us adequately. Blessed assurance will indeed be of some benefit to us oftentimes, but alone will not always suffice in the bitter, stark, unfairness of our reality in the worrisome world in which we must live and work.

It is quite understandable, really, to cling resolutely to a firm belief in the certainty of assurance. Who among us does not keenly realize past or present situations when we would openly welcome words of assurance offered in a timely way. We all sometimes arrive at that point of anxious dread where a fear of ambiguity in some circumstance can lead to the threat of loss of our sense of personal security: we often feel unable to live with a question mark in daily life. Seeking that quest for steady order in our lives, a coherence about the safe, or somewhat safe, routineness of our days, and a unity amid the noisy clamor and irrational structures of our world seem more than mere goals for which we strive. However, that human quest for truly resolute, hard and fast certitudes toward matters of our faith can actually deprive us of spiritual growth. Since our life experiences are dynamic, a genuinely sustaining faith in religion may require us at times to need new information, to reconsider positions long held frozen in certitude, or to feel free to reformulate ideas to better understand ourselves and our relationships with others and with God. Simply put, there may be other resources available to our spiritual well-being. Then we may perhaps know a maturation of thought further enabling us spiritually to better deal with life's difficult times when the status quo is upset. Of course, it can be terribly intimidating and threatening; sometimes sudden changes or new ideas are to be resisted or avoided at all costs because our normal sense of security is uncomfortably shaken. However, instead of the sure clinging to that resolute claim of "blessed assurance," our attention might instead be drawn to a notion of tentativeness. In the hymn "Lead, Kindly Light" we find these words: "I do not ask to see the distant scene; one step enough for me."[41]

Your life, my life and the lives of those around us all contain some uncertainties. Somehow we must recognize that the unknowable, unpredictable and the mysterious of life are simply components of the mix of our reality, or even of "normal lives." Jesus himself, the biblical account informs us, was not immune from this component: the night before he selected his close disciples was spent in totally fervent, thoughtful prayer to

---

[41] Cardinal Newman, "Hymn," *Concise Dictionary of Religious Quotations*, comp. William Neil (Grand Rapids: Eerdmans, 1974) 127.

God the Father regarding his decisions. Afterward, Jesus included the betrayer Judas among his disciples! The uncertainties of life are around us all, forcing us to accept that tentativeness of our faith, one step at a time. We will get to that distant scene in time, but for now, one step, first.

Another example drawn from the New Testament provides us with an account of the forerunner of Jesus Christ, the bold presenter of the great Advent hope, one known as John the Baptist. He was the figure pointing to the coming of Christ's ministry, soon to happen. He was the one who dispensed with the accessories of comfortable life, insisting on his bold, plain speaking from the open spaces of the desert. John expected and vividly advocated the coming of Christ in a bold and charismatic fashion — he announced that with Christ's coming, there would be a prompt and forceful overthrow of the wicked from their power, and a quick vindication of the righteous. There came a point, however, where even this strongly assertive forerunner, so very confident with his message, began to doubt his own words. Key changes were not evident — his idea of Christ had not yet come, the powerful and wicked ruler Herod was still in charge, and the morally disturbing status quo remained undisturbed. And if they were not enough, John himself was placed under arrest and cast into Herod's prison.

It was from his prison cell that John the Baptist sent a question to Jesus: "Are you the one who is to come, or are we to wait for another?" (Matthew 11:3) The biblical writer affords us this look, the now centuries-old account of the assertive proponent boldly preaching the expectant news, and then in his times of dire personal difficulty expressing his own questions regarding those very newsworthy events about which he himself so fervently preached. The biblical account also includes Jesus' patient and understanding response to John's question — not a chastening rebuke, reprimand, or accusation of his apparent lack of faith, but rather a noteworthy reflective acknowledgment of John's genuine faith struggle. The account has Jesus' words this way: "A greater than John the Baptist has not risen." Jesus did not chasten him for lack of faith: surely, we all can draw much solace and comfort from this story of human tentativeness in faithful struggles.

Struggles in personal faith, of course, have indeed entered lives from centuries ago on up to our present age, sparing perhaps no one among us. Sometimes one's very spirit seems at stake as the heaviness of the moment may feel more than one can bear. In the awful heaviness of the most difficult moments in our lives, we fully realize that the once pleasant status quo can suddenly or drastically turn. Often, it is actually unbelievable. Our encounters with the tormenting, unwanted components of human living try our souls and greatly test our faith. Life experiences span a wide and vast spectrum, covering such extremes of good and ill. Yet ambiguities of life need not paralyze us, stopping us dead-in-our-tracks — for we are on a journey. As we continue walking toward the greatest goal, that eternal relationship of love with Eternal God, we are indeed able to courageously keep our focus steadily onward. Even though we simply do not have real control over the *fact* of our human existence, we absolutely possess firm and steadfast control over the *meaning* of our human lives, the all-important and significant meaning which cannot be taken away ever. Our journey onward is the drive thrusting us ahead. As long as we keep that divine goal close to the human heart, we can deal with what life presents us. This is our hope in God. Taking one day at a time, we continue walking on our journey. "I do not ask to see the distant scene; one step enough for me."

CHAPTER 23

ACCESS TO KNOWING

How can we have a genuine faith in such a vast God? If Creator God is so immense and awesome, all-knowing, all-powerful and all-present, how can we mere mortals even relate? How are we to fathom even some understanding of such a God as this? Possibly, we are doing the best we can.

God's being does in fact appear to be a much larger concept than we can manage. Century after century of religious history has attested to many instances of poor management of a workable, coherent understanding of how God and humans relate. It might be said that we at times have seemed even to mismanage what aspects of God's being we do grasp. Often we may appear to prefer a smaller, more usable concept of God which we can more easily digest. We cannot, though, truly contain genuinely workable concepts of God in rather small, inadequate areas of content which do little to illustrate the utter vastness of such a magnificently expansive, universal presence of being. Maybe we can somehow try to do better.

God has wondrously allowed us much knowledge of God's being in relationships with humanity as written down in Scriptures, the Bible. The Scriptures provide a wealth of understanding. Yet, the biblical variety and richness of spirit are so vast that it appears we can and have become overwhelmed by all of it. Regrettably, some apparent differences and inconsistencies in the variety within its pages have produced great rifts and rival voices among many of the faithful followers. Many pastors and theologians alike argue violently among themselves about differing interpretations and viewpoints on God's revealed material. Oftentimes the rifts are regrettable and most embarrassing. Rude, impolite arguments from whatever corner do very little to convey God's loving care that God wishes we offer in our relationships among ourselves.

God trusts us with this knowledge. By offering us much written scriptural knowledge to utilize in our lives, to better develop our moral compass to chart our lifelong course, God trusts us to be wise. God provides for the sustenance of our faith and hope. God's intentions would seem to have us accept this vast amount of material which was surely meant to be more a book of faith and hope than merely a history book — this we can assume. Certainly any instances of historical errors should not in themselves shatter our faith — but possibly we can be shrewd enough to realize that human writers do make human errors, always have and probably always will.

> If we believe that God overruled and inspired the record of those events upon which faith depends, then it is right to suppose that such an account should be reliable. Clearly an inspired Bible is a reliable Bible. But does this reliability necessarily extend to every single detail?
>
> It is important to keep a sense of proportion here. Some might think the discovery of one inaccuracy, however small, in any part of the Bible would cast doubt on everything else in the Bible. But this is clearly not the case. Bible truth is rich and strong: it is not fragile like a gas balloon — one prick and the whole thing crashes to the ground.
>
> Many problems also arise through failing to appreciate the variety of writings in the Bible. Much of the Bible is poetry, proverb, challenge, warning — writings that appeal directly to the imagination, the heart, the conscience. Their impact and the way in which they are true will be very different from that of the historical writings in the Bible. And even the historical writings contain poetic and symbolic elements that are not intended to be a straightforward record of events.[42]

Perhaps we can step back a bit to view all of what God has bestowed for us as resources. God provides us so much. Other factors as well may be beneficial to us: experience, revelation, tradition, culture and reason in addition to Scripture if considered together (though with varying levels) might

---

[42] Walter Moberly, "The Place of the Bible," *Eerdman's Handbook to Christian Belief*, ed. Robin Keeley (Grand Rapids: Wm. B. Eerdman's Publishing Co., 1982), 183.

allow us to more easily avoid distortions and exaggerations in forming our understanding of religious content.[43] Valued life experiences of faith have always been complicated, and a truly meaningful development of our understanding of our faith will naturally be complex as well. We probably can expect no different. To come to a better workable understanding of our God's relation with us by solely relying on one book, the Bible, or any one book for that matter, as our only resource at hand is to deny the vastness of God's great being and all of what God has offered us and is offering us still today. Should we limit ourselves needlessly? We know God seems limitless. It seems God is and has always been a much bigger concept than we can manage. An all-knowing, all-powerful and all-present God obviously cannot be limited in content or contained by merely one book, even if that one book is the Bible, its vastness notwithstanding. As a vital and holy book of hope, it stands as an absolutely necessary component of faith which Christians require for living of these days, and indeed as a moral compass offering the direction of divine hope for us all. Its unique significance need not be diminished.

By using all of what God has given us, we may further discover meaningful ways by which to truly know God and better relate to others. A genuine faith with Eternal God may require that. We can admit that we have access to several resources at hand: wise use of experience, revelation, Scripture, tradition, culture and reason, taken together in varying degrees, may additionally provide our human yearning a more formative basis for developing a firmer, lasting faith for greater understanding. With the utter vastness of our Creator God and the potential of God's created life, we may indeed choose to utilize all such resources available. Life experiences of faith require so much. Surely God permits us to use many gifts in our yearning for ever stronger faith.

---

[43] Macquarrie 4-19.

CHAPTER 24

2000 AD AND BEYOND

What kind of future will there be for us here on this planet of ours? What on earth is going to happen? Do we have any idea of what things will be like? Can we discover any answers today about tomorrow? Questions, we have. Answers? We can all offer some.

When we speak of future events here on earth, we know many will instantly think of those widely popular notions of the psychic realm, that is, the world of extrascientific phenomena, the realm which has given us Bermuda Triangle mysteries, Bigfoot legends and the Loch Ness monster. Television and magazines loudly and generously present that psychic world which offers us great excitement from amazing and illusive subjects. Insofar as God's relationship with us is concerned, our future on earth does involve the spiritual side of our being; this fact, of course, we cannot deny. Our spiritual relating to a spiritual Being, however, involves true, genuine effects upon our real lives here in the real world as we ourselves experience them. Our faith in God through belief in Jesus as Christ is not subject to the psychic realm of extrascientific phenomena. Fortune tellers, astrologers and others who claim inexplicable abilities to perceive or influence events oftentimes gather many fervent believers. Regrettably, the reality is more akin to tricksters preying upon the most gullible among us. The Eternal God, as the loving, caring Maker-of-us-all, understands this gullible tendency, and surely encourages us to be steadfast and to beware. We can accept that certainly our Creator God wishes for us to utilize all our God-given resources of logic and basic common sense to dispel notions of magical thinking away from our spiritual life — to separate that which offers real hope from that which offers, let us say, fame and fortune. Ultimately, fortune tellers will enrich their own lives, materially; whereas, tellers of our Creator God will enrich the lives of all who believe, spiritually. If we can stay focused in our minds upon these differences, we can indeed stay better focused upon our future with God.

In looking upon the future on earth, we first realize we live in the stream of time as we experience it — namely, past, present and future. Also, we know that time was created whenever the Creator fashioned the universe into being, as time is actually measured by the movement of the planet Earth spinning (for our day) and orbiting all around the sun (for our year); both are huge heavenly bodies which the Creator created many eons ago. Time was created by the Eternal Being, who is above time and beyond time. As the maker of time and space our Creator God fashioned this system for us to journey through, to live our lifetimes in the context of what God provided us to experience. As our own individual human journeys are measured in a lifetime of years, we increasingly tend with age to concern ourselves with matters of time. Often, we dwell on the past and often we do the same on our future. Upon reflection, we might readily agree that time is actually an artificial way of understanding the duration between what we refer to as the past, through our present and then on into our future. Well aware that what just a mere moment ago was the present has slipped on into the past and thereby is no longer present, we understand how time can appear so "slippery" and how it can seem to just fly by. The stream of time is like that; and the future comes quickly into the present. We exist actually in the only real time, our present. Past can be thought of as our present memory of yesterdays; and, the future can be thought of as our present-moment expectation of tomorrows ahead.

Humans and God are affected differently with the time stream: the Creator God, who began this system of ours, is unlimited in time and is simply not bound by this system, whereas we, who are quite limited with time, are certainly bound by this system. We move and have our being in the stream of time. In a mere passing of a second, our future comes ever closer at hand into our present. In essence, the future on earth is practically upon us already.

As we attempt to set the scene for considering the future, we now possibly can gather perspective from just how the once-present slipped away to become the past. In other words, perhaps we can wonder if in studying our past events we can thereby project, or even predict somehow further ahead along the time stream, into future events. Those among us who study history, in the vital tasks of accurately recording human events, realize this is a risky venture fraught with dangers: to project ahead would most certainly require at least a sound and reliable basis upon which to rely. We can easily surmise that weak foundations of study inevitably end with weak results of conclusion. As events or changes in the time stream happen, humans take note and the historians among us carefully record and study, for our history's sake. In the immense book *History of the World*, the historian J. M. Roberts offers these words near the book's end. "Only two general truths emerge from the study of history. One is that things tend to change much more, and more quickly, than one might think. The other is that they tend to change much less, and much more slowly, than one might think." So we can consider that to predict is probably too risky to attempt safely. This contemporary historian also makes the case for avoiding prophecy, as he points out that the historian's subject matter is really the past.[44] Thus, our human dilemma in the attempt to set the scene for considering the future: as humans are both responsible beings and are free to behave either responsibly or irresponsibly, the history of future events cannot yet be written, as we just do not know how those with power and influence will behave and treat their fellow humans. We simply do not know. What we do know for sure is that the time stream is a quick one as the future so soon becomes the present and, after the very slightest instant, then becomes the past. This is the undeniable characteristic of the system of time which the Creator God created for us.

Presently in the very late stages of the twentieth century, we human beings appear to exhibit an inordinate amount of fascination and genuine interest in the coming year of 2000 in particular, and also the next millennium in general. Because of this fact of calendar, interesting reactions are occurring all around us. Rising expectations can often appear to mount to such a feverish intensity as to seemingly acquire a life of their own: two opposing viewpoints now appear to be crystallizing regarding the good or bad which will befall us, just ahead now over the horizon of time. Some point to something akin to *Hell-on-earth*, let us say, with dire predictions of utterly bad repercussions for humanity's safety and survival; whereas others point to

---

[44] Roberts, 922, 914.

Heaven-on-earth, shall we say, with fervent hope and conviction of Divine intervention into the human scene here on earth. So, the fact of the calendar seems to presently present us with two different and opposing scenarios, such that we may sense the unavoidable compulsion to choose between them, whether we really wish to or not. That future is suddenly at hand.

The future *Hell-on-earth* prospects for humanity appear to have a basis from the apparent facts of human tendency to wantonly self-destruct. There seems to be at least four main areas of negative factors which we can readily point to as underlying a basis for human self-destruction. 1) Industrialized countries and also developing countries have contributed to tremendous deterioration of their native environments: numerous instances of inefficient and unsound energy production and use in addition to massive pollution problems have resulted in much of the world destroying the very air, water and land we need for our earthly survival. If left unchecked, we will be our own undoing. Should these developments not cause dire harm to our own generation of inhabitants on this planet, the next generation might inherit the consequences of our generation's folly. 2) Another unfortunate aspect of our human destruction (as if that already listed were not enough) is the awesome degree of production, sales and stockpiling of a vast array of military hardware and weapons of all description. Many of us fear that with the technological advances of our modern age we humans have generated further sophisticated weapons of mass destruction, including nuclear, chemical and biological munitions, such that the number of countries with access to, possession and use of such doomsday mechanisms has grown larger as each year goes by. Several of these countries have long-standing, deep national disagreements and disputes with each other, some with a history of wars and violent border clashes. So, it may be believed these violent capabilities loom larger with such advanced weaponry of massive scale. Human worries, based on these developments, are great. The dangers are very real, and they cannot be "sugar-coated" or satisfactorily diminished in their potential degree of destruction, if unleashed. 3) Our own human inhumanity shown to others around us, in an individual scale (as opposed to the larger, governmental scale just listed), such as the apparently widespread acceptance of the use of violence to settle disputes and disagreements. This can easily be seen in the phenomenal accessibility of handguns, for example, in many societies and countries. Most often we hear of the consequences being heartbreaking to strangers, neighbors, friends and family members. Not only wrongdoing to others, but also intolerance of different views or petty disagreements over inconsequential matters can and do wind up as factors in someone's decision to use firearms to settle scores or seek satisfaction in revenge. Heart-rending tragedies are the results, leaving many years of real grief and suffering and fierce pain in the wake. 4) It seems that hunger and poverty have always been a part of the human condition, for recorded history has continually informed us of this fact. At any given time, there is not just one but even several distant people or countries in the world truly suffering with either a real shortage of food or of adequate and basic necessities for shelter and clothing. Generally, the consequences may involve unsuitable living conditions, which in turn contribute to horrible health dilemmas further triggering outbreaks of diseases. We know that major organizations and nations of goodwill have historically garnered energy to alleviate areas of suffering where possible (if not hindered by warring armies in the midst of conflicts, as is often the case). Yet, the needs appear to grow on such a scale as to overwhelm the capacities of resources and logistics to deliver help quickly. In summary, these four examples of factors are regrettably a part of who we are on this earth at this time. The extent we humans experience a Hell-on-earth may ultimately depend on our own acceptance of responsible stewardship of this created world and of the created life in us all, given to us by the Creator God. The repercussions of irresponsible actions by human hands will be too horrific to contemplate. Today the voices of the growing numbers of victims are rarely heard.

It can be said that it is in the tormenting context of such depressing scenes of today's world that a Hell-on-earth scenario for humanity's near future gains acceptance. Many say that our world will surely be an unfit habitat for any life, as humankind's tendency to self-destruct probably will continue then as it has evidenced itself in the past — in other words that Hell, right here on this earth, will be unavoidable. In addition, even if there would be any surviving human population of our doomsday making, the anxiety alone of the situation at hand would be intolerable to say the least. A half century ago, before such talk of doomsday became commonplace, the renowned psychologist Rollo May wrote these words regarding what most of us, in an ordinary life, may encounter.

> The evidence is overwhelming ... that we live today in an "age of anxiety." If one penetrates below the surface ... one runs athwart the problem of anxiety at almost every turn. The ordinary stresses and strains of life in the changing world of today are such that few if any escape the need to confront anxiety and to deal with it in some manner.[45]

Add to this picture of 1950 the vast extent to which the world has changed since then in terms of modern weaponry's technological advances, for example, and it would no doubt cause even the most casual of observers to feel anxious and depressed. In such troubling context, many say the world simply will not survive the year 2000 AD, that the dangers are too awesome, plentiful and deadly for humankind to control in any manner — the conclusion being that the year 2000 will be it! That will be the year in which it is all over for human beings! It is as simple as that; simple to see, simple to foresee.

It was said that on the first anniversary of his election as pope, Pope John XXIII mentioned that a man of his age, 78, did not have much of a future left. Not only did John XXIII have a good deal of future left, he would accomplish much to alter the entire face of the Catholic Church through the Second Vatican Council. At the opening of the council, Pope John spoke these words:

> In these modern times, they can see nothing but prevarication and ruin. They say that our era, in comparison with past eras, is getting worse. And they behave as though they learned nothing from history, which is nonetheless the teacher of life. ... We feel that we must disagree with those prophets of doom, who are always forecasting disaster as though the end of the world were at hand. ... In the present order of things, Divine Providence is leading us to a new order of human relations.[46]

Those persons holding viewpoints of *Heaven-on-earth* prospects for the future actually emphasize much the same trends of human folly. However, the crucial difference for this perspective of our future is that the prediction extends further to point out that God would obviously intervene before humankind destroys itself completely. In this, the conviction of many is firm

---

[45] Rollo May, *The Meaning of Anxiety* (New York: Washington Square Press, 1979) xv.
[46] Woodeene Koenig-Bricker, *365 Saints: Your Daily Guide to the Wisdom and Wonder of Their Lives* (San Francisco: Harper Collins 1995) November 25.

and steadfast. Also from this view, many affirm that obviously the year 2000 is simply and ultimately of great significance to God, for God is absolutely going to intervene in that year with the second coming of Christ into this world! Many pastors have charted out specifics of God's plans within their individual churches to point when God is actively saving the believers from humanity's self-destruction: the spiritually climactic year 2000, when God triumphantly enters, is around the corner! The fact of the calendar alone informs us the climax of 2000 AD is virtually upon us, ready or not.

As regards the truly momentous (and historically significant) milestone of reaching another millennium, whereby we in any ordinary year in early January, in our daily personal business, have to get used to saying and writing a different number for the new year — in this case, the year 2000 will be different altogether from what we are used to. Such a major change is indeed historic, awesome to contemplate — 2000 AD.

Most of us recall that the calendar which most of our world goes by has the traditional endings BC (meaning "Before Christ") and AD (meaning *Anno Domini*, or Latin for "year of the Lord"). The year of the birth of Jesus Christ is the central event in relation to which historical time-reckoning is calculated and updated the world over. Therefore, the year 2000 is considered the two-thousandth year after Jesus was born — and thus the great significance of a major milestone in human history! The exact dates of Jesus' life, though, are still uncertain; however, it is virtually certain that he was not born in the year 1, as was traditionally held. That traditional year of Jesus' birth was determined in calculations by a sixth century monk in Rome, named Dionysius Exiguus — but he made an error in the calculations which placed the date several years off. No adjustment was ever made. At the present time, the general scholarly opinion (also taking into account the years of King Herod's rule) tends to favor a date about 7 BC.[47] The mathematical consequences of an error of that degree therefore places the actual 2,000th year after the birth of Jesus at about the year 1993 or 1994, instead of 2000! As this is the case, were God to act decisively, boldly, by sending the second coming of Christ on behalf of the believers in the all-important 2,000th year after Jesus' birth — well, God apparently missed it, since that 2,000th year

---

[47] John Macquarrie, *Mediators Between Human and Divine* (New York: Continuum, 1996) 103, 162.

has already come and gone! We humans have already reached that milestone: most of us without even realizing that was the case. We have reached that year, and others beyond it, and God has yet to have Christ's return come about. For all we know, God may still direct it to happen in the year 2000 by our calendar, though it will in actuality be about 2,007 years after Jesus' birth. For those who boldly pronounce the year 2000 as singularly significant as the year Eternal God will send forth Christ's return to our earth, the facts of our calendar have already shown them wrong, in the sense of the 2,000th year. Actually, loud or prominent voices may be wrong for the specific year of 2000 or for *any specific year* predicted, for that matter, according to biblical accounts. "But about that day or hour no one knows, neither the angels in heaven, nor the Son, but only the Father." (Mark 13:32) "It is not for you to know the times or periods that the Father has set by his own authority." (Acts 1:7)

The human community truly knows very little of the *timing of events* in our future. Only God knows, it would seem. Nor do we really know in absolute confidence the *specific nature* of future events, for we simply cannot make bold claims with absolutely accurate premonition. Of these, we have to admit our finitude, our limited human nature. We may not know what the future holds, yet we can indeed know who holds the future — in other words, the Eternal God in divine providence will bring about the kingdom of God in God's own timing, in God's own ways.

What then can we say of our appropriate response to the year of 2000 AD? Perhaps it should be best considered as another year to continue on in the work at hand. The work for us all is great. As was listed earlier, the factors contributing much to the anxiety before us are heavy indeed: human worries are real, the dangers before us are great. "Of all the unpleasant emotions anxiety probably ranks as the most common. All humans experience it at times. . . . Our present age is still often described as 'the age of anxiety'."[48]

One writer, P. T. Chandapilla, described the setting of particular economic and social conditions today in India, a country beset with truly great hardships for humankind there:

---

[48] Dale Simpson, "Anxiety," *Baker Encyclopedia of Psychology*, ed. David G. Benner (Grand Rapids: Baker Book House, 1985) 64-65.

> Fifty per cent (of the population of India) live below the poverty line, meaning they have less than one simple meal of a bowl of rice and a soup of lentils, every twenty-four hours. Their clothing and shelter are of no consequence below this line. When you add to those below the poverty line those who are just poor, they amount to eighty per cent of the present population. This percentage continues to increase because the explosion in population growth is at its greatest in the lower economic level. Coupled with this is the selfishness of the acquisitive twenty per cent, the "haves" over against the "have nots."[49]

Another writer recounts the story of Mother Teresa, the renowned figure of tireless personal service to the very poorest of the poor.

> Walking through Calcutta one day, Mother Teresa came across what appeared to be a bundle of rags on the pavement. Upon closer inspection, it turned out to be a woman, barely conscious, her face partially eaten away by rats and ants. Mother Teresa and another nun lifted the woman and took her to a hospital. The hospital refused to accept her, saying that there were no beds; besides, the woman was dying, there was nothing to be done. When Mother Teresa asked where they might take her, she was told that they should return her to the place where they had found her. Mother Teresa refused to leave, and she was with the woman when she died a few hours later. "It was then that I decided to find a place for the dying and take care of them myself," she later said.[50]

It may seem as if the world is comprised of anxiety-laden situations resulting in dire hardships for teeming masses of people. Possibly it can be surmised that the dire, depressing hardships in which some find themselves caught oftentimes become the very places which others willingly choose for service. Such was obviously the case with Mother Teresa. Recognition of genuine human need can indeed instill a firm resolve to meet our universal human responsibilities, however trying and difficult. Perhaps these are, as well, the very places God would have us consider in assessing our future here on earth; for the stream of time is also the stream of humanity — those before us, those presently, and those who come afterwards. A contemporary philosopher gives us these words as part of an affirmation of human unity:

---

[49] P. T. Chandapilla, "Life-Style Today," *Eerdman's Handbook to Christian Belief*, ed. Robin Keeley (Grand Rapids: Wm. B. Eerdman's Publishing Co., 1982), 365.
[50] Abraham Verghese, "Last Acts," *The New Yorker* September 22, 1997: 80.

> All our deeds affect the human future, as the life of each of us has in its turn been affected by those who have lived before us. . . . We are not monadic individuals, but mutually interacting parts of the one human world in which the thoughts and acts of each reverberate continually for good or ill through the lives of others. As the ways in which men and women have lived in the past have formed the world in which we now have to live, so we in turn are now forming the world in which future generations will have to dwell. . . . The world today is such that if we do not unite in a common life, we are only too likely, to find ourselves united in a common death.[51]

As we reflect and consider the future of earth and fully affirm the imperative for continual efforts in human unity amid such an anxiety-producing array of hardships in our world, we discover that individually we cannot, as Rollo May put it, "escape the need to confront anxiety and to deal with it in some manner." If ever-real perils, evermore powerful, are seemingly multiplying around us, then we might very well conclude this "age of anxiety" will continue from the present into our future. Like it or not, we are forced to deal with it in some manner.

> Now it is right that we should think about the future, and it is a very foolish person who does not think about it at all. But what we are always warned against in Scripture is about being worried about the future. . . . Thinking is right up to a point, but if you go beyond that point it becomes worry and anxiety and it paralyzes and cripples. In other words, although it is very right to think about the future, it is very wrong to be controlled by it. . . . It is a waste of time to be concerned about the past which you cannot affect; but it is equally wrong to be worried about the future which at the moment is obscure. "One step enough for me." Live in the present to the maximum and do not let your future mortgage your present any more than you should let the past mortgage your present.[52]

Additional practical observations regarding how we can consider those burdens of future which weigh upon us are offered by still other authors:

> Focus on *today* as the present, to find meaning within that time frame. This approach is valid and wise. None of us control our future, nor live in it. Nor can we live in the past. God gives us the present in which to live, and it is in

---

[51] John H. Hick, *Philosophy of Religion* (Englewood Cliffs: Prentice-Hall, 1983) 143.
[52] D. Martyn Lloyd-Jones, *Spiritual Depression: Its Causes and Its Cure* (Grand Rapids: Eerdmans, 1984) 98-99.

> our present that life is to have meaning and purpose. It is also in the present that we can know the comfort of God's love. 'Surely I will be with you always' is the Scripture's great reminder that, as we move through time, we never reach a present in which we are isolated from God's love.
>
> The Christian is convinced that each human being has an eternal destiny. Human life is too significant to God, and individuals made in His image are too highly valued, to fade away to nothingness. Human personality and self-consciousness continue beyond the death of the body. . . . The promise of God's presence in our present, in the immediate future, and forever, is a reality that gives both life and death unique meaning.[53]

Since we can easily visualize the future as something of an extension of the present, in as much as time may be viewed as something akin to a stream moving on by, we truly find it acceptable thinking to live each day unto itself. To focus upon today only, as it is the only day in which we live anyway, is to take one day at a time. We cannot live in any future day, except when it later on becomes our present. Biblical perspective can also be found touching upon our living in the present (from Matthew 6:26,28,34).

> Look at the birds of the air; they neither sow nor reap nor gather into barns, and yet your heavenly Father feeds them. Are you not of more value than they? . . . Consider the lilies of the field, how they grow; they neither toil nor spin. . . . So do not worry about tomorrow, for tomorrow will bring worries of its own. Today's trouble is enough for today.

This present day is really all that we now know for sure God is giving to us: we cannot absolutely count on more days, though we certainly want to assume there will be more ahead. If we carry this idea further, by leaving aside those other cares for tomorrow, the realization may happen that we will focus more on experiencing God in the here-and-now. Then maybe we can actually find meaningful experience with God even in the commonplace and the routine of our day. That awesome encounter with God that Moses experienced was in the very common, usual context of his daily work, caring for flocks of sheep.

One conclusion we might draw from our focus upon the future on this earth is that our perspective is the key to it all. To change our capacity to

---

[53] Richards and Johnson 116-117.

perceive time itself is to adjust ourselves within our relationships with God and with others. To make such a change in our perspective is to consider all things new again, even old notions developed years and years ago. Reflecting upon past assumptions made about the present might allow us the freedom to reconsider aspects of our relationships with others, our relationship with God, and quite possibly, even our very conception of God. In the book *Anatomy of Faith* by Rabbi Milton Steinberg, we can find these words:

> "God" does not denote an old man on a throne somewhere up in the sky. That notion is in part a survival of the infancy of the human race, in part a hangover from our personal childhood, from those days when, having first heard about God and possessing only limited intellectual resources, we pictorialized Him according to our naiveté. . . . To believe in God, maturely, intelligently, is to believe that reality did not just "happen," that it is no accident, no pointless interplay of matter and energy. . . . It is to hold that the universe, physical and moral, is a cosmos, not an anarchy — made a cosmos instead of an anarchy, meaningful rather than mad, because it is the manifestation of a creating, sustaining, animating, design-lending Spirit, a Mind-will, or to use the oldest, most familiar and best word, a God.[54]

As our intimate relationship with God appears to be the all-important, ultimate relationship we have, we can fully realize that there indeed existed reasons why the Creator God created each of us. We are individuals, meaning each is uniquely different from all others on this planet — and yet, all of us on this planet were made in the image of God. Only through the awesome power and awesome love of Creator God was this possible. It surely happened by design, not by accident, that the Creator provided each of us with our own unique, novel personality — each a special being but with the same capacity as everyone else to love God and others. Perhaps the most logical reason God started life as we know it was to create for God's love novel beings for an eternal relationship: God, an infinite and personal Being, has as many different relationships with us as there are human beings created. Each different person relates with that person's Creator in a varying manner, even though we all are still made in the Creator's image. In *Leaves of Grass*, Walt Whitman expressed these thoughts:

---

[54] Milton Steinberg, *Anatomy of Faith* (New York: Harcourt Brace, 1960) 88-89.

> I see something of God each hour of the twenty-four, and each moment then,
> In the faces of men and women I see God, and in my own face in the glass;
> I find letters from God dropped in the street, and every one is signed by God's name,
> And I leave them where they are, for I know that others will punctually come forever and ever.[55]

As we grow up into this world we mature in our relationships with God, and surely God expects for us to do likewise in our other relationships also. The Creator God began our humankind with divine love and care, and we are a part of God's process of creation as we extend the love and care outward to others around us.

> This creative process of God will culminate in God's final novelty, the Creation of a new world. Glimpses of a new creation have been foreshadowed in the life and destiny of Jesus Christ and continue to be seen in God's present involvement in the world. God's caring attitude toward humanity, however, does not dismiss humans from their position as God's administrators. Through the example and sign of hope, God has established in Jesus Christ, he invites them to participate in his own care, both for their fellow human beings, and for the rest of creation. Only by experiencing that someone cares with infinite compassion for us finite beings, do we become truly human beings. We are free to care for others with the same intensity as we would care for ourselves. . . . Only from the one who provides our existence with origin as well as with structure do we obtain an understanding of our journey. We realize that we are not helplessly and hopelessly adrift in space and time. . . . There is purpose and direction in the universe. . . . The experience of a God who cares endows our existence with meaning, and, at the same time, permits us to understand the whole world as God's creation. The world was not created for our exploitation or self-glorification. Our uniquely human position notwithstanding, the cosmos was created together with us to enjoy God and to be enjoyed by him forever.[56]

Such a wondrous relationship with God, and hopefully also with others around us, can possibly develop into the greatest hope which we humans have. We fully acknowledge that a true meaning and purpose to our lives unavoidably involves the context of our time spent here on earth: a lifetime of

---

[55] Walt Whitman, "Leaves of Grass," *The Harper American Literature*, ed. Donald McQuade, vol. 1 (New York: Harper & Row, 1987) 2375.
[56] Schwarz 268-269.

moments provide our opportunities for meaning. The Creator God graciously gave us all our own personal lifetimes — lifetimes big enough and varied enough for each to experience numerous possible opportunities to explore life in all of its richness. Meaning and purpose are available to all. We can catch signals of this from the thoughts expressed in the New Testament passage of Ecclesiastes 3:1-8.

> For everything there is a season,
> and a time for every matter under heaven:
>
> a time to be born, and a time to die;
> a time to plant, and a time to pluck up what is planted;
> a time to kill, and a time to heal;
> a time to break down, and a time to build up;
> a time to weep, and a time to laugh;
> a time to mourn, and a time to dance;
> a time to throw away stones, and a time to gather stones together;
> a time to embrace, and a time to refrain from embracing;
> a time to seek, and a time to lose;
> a time to keep, and a time to throw away;
> a time to tear, and a time to sew;
> a time to keep silence, and a time to speak;
> a time to love, and a time to hate;
> a time for war, and a time for peace.

A certain sense of rhythm is detected within these lines from the ancient account of time in our lives. The ebb and flow of thoughts provide us with this sense. As the biblical writer of old stresses to us that there exists a season for everything and a time for every matter under heaven, pulsating references to time come beating regularly to our hearing. This probably is by design, rather than by accident, intended to offer us a full effect. The ancient writer possessed an awareness of pulsing rhythm. We can say that humans centuries ago, humans today, and all human beings in time, in fact, possess inside them beating reminders of regularity. The physical heart allows us this time to live. Also should we "find the time" to be still with a moment or two of quiet solitude, we will discover anew the rhythm of time within our being.

Regrettably, we live in the fast-paced days of an age of anxiety, usually much too preoccupied with our worries to notice this orderly and periodic essence of our personal lifetimes, our past-present-future continuum, our stream of time. Through our living within the stream of time, even the most uncertain of times, God has been there with us, like the beating heart. So we recall the Divine assurance: "I will be with you always." Seldom noticed like our beating hearts, the Creator God's rhythm of abundant life has been thriving all along and all around us. God's gift of time has allowed this rhythm. (Also from the book of Ecclesiastes, 1:5-7)

> The sun rises and the sun goes down, and hurries to the place where it rises. The wind blows to the south, and goes around to the north; round and round goes the wind, and on its circuits the wind returns. All streams run to the sea, but the sea is not full; to the place where the streams flow, there they continue to flow.

CHAPTER 25

WALKING

You are walking. You come alongside the fence which encloses a piece of wooded land which dips low enough for you to see the top of some of the trees there. Evidence of life abounds in front of you. You can see and hear this evidence. The effects of the soft breeze upon the branches are displayed in the gentle swaying of the leaves and proclaimed in their steady rustling noises. You sense you actually hear plant life. Then you realize this steady rustling is merely a backdrop, a constant background music for the intermittent sounds of various bird calls originating from somewhere within these trees. Then you know you also hear animal life. You enjoy coming along this fence; you have walked along it many times recently.

Suddenly you recall from a few days ago a bird constructing a nest, and how it was gone the next day after a heavy overnight rainstorm and violent winds.

It's there, right there, through that section of branches that your attention is drawn. The leaves are a gathered mix of light and dark greens, those lightened by sunlight and those darkened by shade from other leaves, a marbled mix of light and dark green coloring.

It's there, right there! You notice a small, delicate-looking bird building a nest at that same narrow-wedged fork of a limb. You also hear the sounds of that activity. For several moments you effortlessly witness that bird arranging its nest with short, tiny twigs, flying in one at a time, carefully pressing each down into its clump of twigs to fasten it all securely together. Questions come. Is this the same bird? Is this the same little bird you noticed and studied a few days before? Is it the same one whose nest was apparently torn away by the storm's fury? You are not really sure. For a moment, you ponder. Then, you realize that you want to believe it is the same one. It's there, right there.

You enjoy walking alongside this fence.

You continue walking.